GIRL TALK: MONEY

girl talk: money

ARIANA MANGUM

Advantage.

Published by Advantage, Charleston, South Carolina.
Member of Advantage Media Group.

ADVANTAGE is a registered trademark, and the Advantage colophon is a trademark of Advantage Media Group, Inc.

Printed in the United States of America.

10 9 8 7 6 5 4 3 2 1

ISBN: 978-1-64225-173-9
LCCN: 2020901936

Cover and layout design by Danna Mathias.

This publication is designed to provide accurate and authoritative information in regard to the subject matter covered. It is sold with the understanding that the publisher is not engaged in rendering legal, accounting, or other professional services. If legal advice or other expert assistance is required, the services of a competent professional person should be sought.

Advantage Media Group is proud to be a part of the Tree Neutral® program. Tree Neutral offsets the number of trees consumed in the production and printing of this book by taking proactive steps such as planting trees in direct proportion to the number of trees used to print books. To learn more about Tree Neutral, please visit **www.treeneutral.com**.

Advantage Media Group is a publisher of business, self-improvement, and professional development books and online learning. We help entrepreneurs, business leaders, and professionals share their Stories, Passion, and Knowledge to help others Learn & Grow. Do you have a manuscript or book idea that you would like us to consider for publishing? Please visit **advantagefamily.com** or call **1.866.775.1696**.

To women everywhere. May you find empowerment in this book.

CONTENTS

INTRODUCTION

L ike many young women, I spent the better part of my early
twenties trying to find my purpose in life. I wanted to impact
the world in my own way, but I didn't know how.

I'm a true believer in the dictum "Follow your bliss," and my
bliss beckoned me when I was in college—strangely enough, in an
econ class. Unlike most of my classmates, whose eyes glazed over
whenever they picked up the textbook, I couldn't get enough of the
law of the invisible hand, business cycles, and the efficient market
hypothesis. I was hooked, and I promptly declared myself an econ
major—even though I wasn't sure what I was going to do with it yet.

In my senior year, I took a capital markets class. I needed one more
elective, and the stock market was still something I knew very little
about. It was in that class that I realized so many of the companies—
companies such as Starbucks, Lululemon, and Facebook—whose
products I used every day were publicly traded and that by buying
stock in these companies, I could own a little piece of them. This was

exciting. Now, at the time, I certainly wasn't in the position to invest the little money that I had in the stock market, but I was more than willing to manage the $2 million mock portfolio that our professor had assigned us. And just like that, I was hooked on stocks. I was addicted to the adrenaline rush of watching my stocks rise and fall each day. My path was clear—I was going to work on Wall Street.

I took the first steps toward making that happen the very next semester when I landed a sweet internship at a large investment firm. I didn't even mind that they gave me the grunt work because I knew that I was going to learn a lot and that I was going to get my little foot into a big door—this was a world-renowned firm. When they offered me a full-time job right out of college … well, you could have knocked me over with a feather!

At first, my job was simply to assist the financial advisors in building financial plans for our clients, but I took every opportunity to sit in on planning meetings. I enjoyed testing out various hypothetical scenarios to find the best fit for each client, and I liked the challenge of simplifying overwhelmingly complex financial jargon and making it easy for the client to understand. During this time, I also became a licensed financial advisor, studying for and passing the required regulatory tests.

I had worked hard and accomplished a lot in just a few short years, but as it turned out, this was just the beginning of my path. It was only after I met my husband that my true passion and purpose really revealed itself. We were a great team. We pushed each other to be our best at work and in life. When it came to our jobs, we didn't want to have to answer to anyone, to have to conform to someone else's rules or requirements. We wanted to do things our own way. Our company, Miramontes Capital, was founded just a few years after we first met, and we haven't looked back since. I have my own financial advising firm now, and my interest in entrepreneurship has only increased. In fact, in addition to Miramontes Capital, I've also branched out to start Nummata, an automated online trading platform for younger investors that expertly allocates portfolios at a lower cost.

One thing that has struck me over the years, as a young woman working in finance, is that very few of the clients who walk in the door at my company are like me—young women eager to take control of their financial lives. In my personal life, my friends often confess to me that they don't have the faintest idea how to use their extra income to prepare for their future.

This is what inspired me to write this book. I want to share everything that I've learned and to ignite in you, my reader, the same fire that was stoked in me years ago when I took that first econ class. I feel it's particularly important to give women the lowdown on what's available to them so they have the knowledge they need to make informed financial decisions instead of just avoiding the subject altogether. It's my intention to write a book that's light and fun, that women will actually want to read, with the hope that it will leave them confident and inspired to tackle their finances.

Let this book be your all-inclusive resource, but know that you don't have to read it cover to cover. This book will give you everything you need to handle your finances confidently at all stages of life, but it's very possible—probable even—that some of the chapters may not apply to you. Whether you are climbing the corporate ladder or starting your own business, there's a chapter in here for you. Whether you are getting married and having kids or living the single life, there's a chapter in here for you. And if you want more insight on money, work, and life, you can head over to ArianaMangum.com anytime.

So if you're ready to become a financial whiz, kick back, get comfy, and let's dive in.

Chapter 1

WE ALL NEED A LITTLE BASIC IN OUR LIVES

eing "basic" is never the goal, but sometimes we all need a little of it in our lives. If you were being completely honest with yourself, you'd probably admit that pumpkin spice is delicious, Uggs are hella comfy, and you could probably use some guidance when it comes to finances. So let's get a little bit basic. Regardless of what phase you've reached in your life, the amount of money in your bank account right now, or how much you *wish* was in your bank account, this chapter is for you. The rest of the book will build on everything we cover in this chapter. It's the foundation on which everything else rests, and none of the advice I offer will work if you don't have the foundation down first. Don't worry if you don't 100 percent understand everything in this chapter; it's really just a brief overview. Much of what we cover here will be explained in more detail in the following chapters.

Budget It!

Tackling your finances requires taking a good, hard look at what it actually costs for you to live. When looking at your budget, be honest about your strengths and weaknesses and what you really spend and are able to save on a month-to-month basis.

While I'm never going to tell you how to spend your money, I will offer a few tips on how to think about breaking down your costs so you don't end up renting an apartment that's way out of your price range and having to eat canned beans for a year while you wait for your lease to run out.

With that said, there's no hard-and-fast rule when it comes to budgeting. Perhaps you have a pretty serious shoe addiction and are willing to forgo going to the movies or to concerts to pay for your habit. Maybe you live in a city where rent is crazy high and takes a huge chunk out of your budget, but you ride your bicycle everywhere, thereby saving on transportation expenses (not to mention a gym membership!).

When looking at your budget, be honest about your strengths and weaknesses and what you really spend and are able to save on a month-to-month basis.

The purpose of this guide is to help you make informed decisions about where your money is going so you don't blow your whole paycheck on a fancy dinner the minute it gets deposited into your account.

At the end of the day, there are some general rules of thumb when it comes to budgeting. This handy chart will help you assess what you should be doing with that paycheck each month.

EXPENSE	PERCENT OF YOUR PAYCHECK
Housing	25-35%
Transportation	5-15%
Food	10-15%
Personal care	10-15%
Healthcare	10-15%
Utilities	4-7%
Entertainment	5-7%
Debt/other	7-15%

TRACKING YOUR EXPENSES

If you need a little help getting a sense of how much you actually spend each month, the good news is that, thanks to modern technology, "There's an app for that!" You can connect apps such as Mint or Quicken to your credit card account, and they will conveniently put each of your purchases into a category for you. I particularly like Mint because you can connect it to all your accounts, set up reminders to check bills, and track your spending. You don't have to check it obsessively, but during those first few months of getting a handle on your finances, it will be instrumental in helping you understand just where your money is going!

Do me a favor, and set this up right now! It only takes a few minutes to log on to each of your accounts from the Mint site. Even if you're not ready to tackle your budget (believe me, I get it!), let Mint get to work aggregating your data so that when it's the right time, you'll have the insights you need.

Save It!

So you've finally got an understanding of your expenses, and you've got some extra money burning a hole in your pocket. Wait! Before you go blow all your spare cash on facials and fancy handbags, you should start thinking about saving it!

How much of your paycheck should you be saving? The answer to that question is going to be different for everyone, but generally speaking, if you are able to put 10 percent of your income into savings, that's a great start.

There are a lot of different places you can put your money: in a checking account, in a savings account, under your mattress, or in pickle jars buried in your backyard. But not all places to keep your money are created equal, and what your money does for you while it's in those places varies. It's useful to have all the information about different kinds of accounts even if you don't take advantage of them right now.

CHECKING ACCOUNT

A checking account is an account held by a bank that allows you to put money in and take money out through checks or a debit card. It's the account you use when you want to take cash out of an ATM, pay your bills, or handle any of your day-to-day financial transactions. If you have been attending to your own finances for a while now, the odds are you already have one of these.

SAVINGS ACCOUNT

A savings account, unlike a checking account, accrues a modest amount of interest. They are federally insured, so your money is safe there, but don't quit your day job just yet: most savings accounts have an annual percentage yield (or APY) of about 0.09 percent.[1]

SIX-MONTH EMERGENCY FUND

The first thing you want to do when you're setting up your savings is to establish a six-month emergency fund—a separate savings account where you put away enough savings to cover six months' worth of expenses. If you're lucky, you won't ever have to use these funds, but if you lose your job or start a new business or have to

---

[1] Lauren Perez, "What Is the Average Interest Rate for Savings Accounts?" SmartAsset, February 13, 2019, https://smartasset.com/checking-account/average-savings-account-interest.

take time off for some other kind of emergency, it's reassuring to know that it's there.

First, calculate your expenses for a single month—including bills, debt, and even the small luxuries that you'd hate to go without—and then multiply that by six. That's your target number for this fund. Don't worry too much about other savings accounts until you have reached this target number. Once you've reached that number, you can put the rest of your savings in other places (which we'll get to in a second!), but until then it's important that you work to build up this fund because if something unexpected *does* happen, you don't want to get penalized for withdrawing early from your IRA or 401(k).

HEALTH SAVINGS ACCOUNT/ FLEXIBLE SAVINGS ACCOUNT

If you're employed by a good-sized company, in addition to a 401(k) you may also have an HSA, or a health savings account, that you can contribute to. An HSA is an account to pay for all your health expenses if you have a high-deductible health plan. It's useful, but it's also underutilized, as most people don't even know they have the option to contribute to an HSA. The major benefit of having an HSA is that all the money you contribute goes in pretax and in some cases, your employer will contribute too.

What does that mean? Well, let's say you need a new pair of glasses. You try on a simple, generic $200 frame that looks fine … but then you spot a really stylish pair of Coach glasses for $300, which is a bit out of your price range (which you know because you are budgeting now—good for you!). Now let's say you are in the 35 percent tax bracket. If you make $300 and put it into a savings account, over $100 of that goes right to taxes, leaving you with only about $200 for those generic frames. But if you put that $300 into an HSA, you don't get taxed on that money, which means you can afford those hot designer glasses.

So you see, if you plan to have any health expenses (which you should since an HSA covers a variety of expenses, including prescriptions, birth control, copays for doctor and dental visits, flu shots, vaccines, physical therapy, acupuncture, and chiropractic care), an HSA is just a smart idea.

Similar to an HSA is an FSA, or a flexible savings account. These are similar, but there are a few key differences.

HSA	FSA
must have a high-deductible health plan	no specification
contribution limit	contribution limit
unused balances roll over	unused balances may roll over
pretax contributions	pretax contributions

An FSA is sort of like an HSA junior. It doesn't require a high-deductible health plan, but oftentimes it has a lower contribution limit, and if you don't use it, it's possible that your unused balance won't roll over to the next year. It's like they say: if you don't use it, you lose it. In the long term, having an account in which your money can roll over and add up over time is definitely an advantage because in your later years, you are likely to have more health expenses than you do now.

If you are self-employed or your employer doesn't offer health insurance, you can still contribute to an HSA. There are just a few eligibility requirements to make note of first: you must be covered under a high-deductible health plan, and no one else can be claiming you as a dependent on their tax returns. I really like Vanguard, as their HSAs contain an investment feature, so the contributions have the ability to make tax-free earnings. Another great feature of Vanguard accounts? If you still have funds in the account at age sixty-five, they don't have to be withdrawn for healthcare expenses. Lastly, there are no required minimum distributions, or RMDs, either. (This is when the Internal Revenue Service [IRS] requires you to start taking withdrawals from your retirement savings if you are not already doing so.).

401(K)

A 401(k) is a retirement savings account offered through your employer. You have the option of putting money in a 401(k) before or after tax. This money is going to be invested on your behalf, and over the years, it will grow. However, it's only to be used after you retire, so you're not allowed to touch it until you're almost sixty. If you do decide to take it out prematurely, you'll be hit with a whopping penalty. Many employers offer some kind of match program—meaning that they'll match some portion of whatever you contribute. Think of it this way: if you aren't contributing, you are pretty much missing out on free money.

IRA/ROTH ACCOUNT

As a general rule, if you're working and making money, you should be contributing to your 401(k). If you have your own business, however, you don't have the luxury of a 401(k). But you should still be saving for retirement, so it's important that you know about your other options—a traditional IRA, an SEP (simplified employee pension) IRA, or a Roth IRA, any of which you can open up at your own bank.

The difference between a traditional IRA and a Roth IRA comes down to when you want to be taxed on it. With a traditional IRA, the deposits you make are tax deductible, but with a Roth IRA, you make your deposits with after-tax earnings. This means that with a traditional IRA, you don't pay taxes when you put your money in, but you're just delaying the inevitable because you are going to eventually pay taxes on that money when you take it out. A Roth IRA gets the messy part of paying taxes out of the way first, so when you finally withdraw that money, it's tax free. Neither is necessarily better or worse than the other, but if you are young and just starting out with your financial life, it's likely that you are in a lower tax bracket than you will be many years later, when you want to withdraw those funds. Because of this, a Roth IRA is probably your best bet.

On the other hand, if you're older and don't expect to be in a high-income bracket when you retire (maybe because you got a late start on saving), a traditional IRA may make more sense. (In fact people above a certain level of income are actually *ineligible* for a Roth IRA!)[2]

As a suggestion I must say I really like Charles Schwab. You can open a checking, savings, and IRA account there (all under one roof is always nice!), and they have competitive trading fees and no ATM fees.

SEP IRAs are for self-employed individuals, and they offer a few additional benefits, such as higher contribution limits than 401(k)s, depending on your take-home pay. As of this writing, the contribution limit is $56,000 per year, or 25 percent of your salary, whichever

---

2   "Which Is Better for Me, a Roth or Traditional IRA?" *CNN Money*, accessed April 24, 2018, http://money.cnn.com/retirement/guide/IRA_Roth.moneymag/index7.htm.

is less. If you decide to grow your business and take on additional employees, your SEP can serve them too; it allows you to make contributions on their behalf. If you're working for a small business that doesn't offer a 401(k), you may be benefiting from an SEP already!

A Warning about Credit

Lots of people I know have made the mistake of thinking that credit is pretty much free money. And I was once one of them. But learning to live within your means, pay back your debt, and maintain good credit is one of the most important financial lessons I can offer, and the earlier you learn it, the better. Trust me, this is coming from a painfully learned experience.

Don't believe me? Here's a little story that I hope serves as a warning against the seemingly endless cash flow of credit.

The moment I turned eighteen, I applied for a credit card. Admittedly, I didn't really understand how credit worked, but I knew you got to buy things now and pay for them somewhere down the line, in some faraway future.

At first, it was great; I'd fill up my gas tank, go out for lunch, and just make the minimum payment each month. I'd find myself at Nordstrom, eyeing a cute Juicy Couture bag that I couldn't afford—before realizing that I could just apply for a Nordstrom charge card and max it out! Which is exactly what I'd do.

But a year later, the thrill had started to wear off. By this point I was in college, I was still working part time … and I was starting to miss payments. I had three or four credit cards, and I couldn't keep track of what was due and when to pay it. I knew there was interest on all these cards, but I didn't really understand how it was calculated or how it added up.

I endured phone call after phone call from debt collection agencies until I finally decided to own up and pay my debt. At the time, my credit score was 350. Three-fifty! Now, for those of you who don't know, 350 isn't just considered bad, it's considered *very bad!* In fact, the scale only goes down to 300. With a score that bad, I couldn't get any credit. No one would give me a credit card, a loan … nothing. So I took it upon myself to read everything I could get my hands on about how to build up my credit. It took me years to build my credit back up, and in that time, I learned a few things about getting and keeping good credit.

ADVICE ON GETTING AND KEEPING GOOD CREDIT

The first, most obvious piece of advice is pay off your balance! Every month, pay it off in full. I know this isn't always an option for everyone, but if it's within your ability, do it!

The second piece of advice is if at all possible, don't exceed 30 percent of your credit limit. Use credit for things you know you can afford and that you can pay back immediately. Once you go over 30 percent of your credit limit, it starts to affect your credit score.

The third piece of advice is keep your old credit cards open and active. Age may be nothing but a number, but it matters for credit cards. If you start out with that standard Capital One card and then move on to a fancier American Express card, keep that Capital One card open. Use it for small purchases, like gas or groceries, and over time the consistency that you've built up with that card will lead to a better credit score.

Fourth, don't actively look for credit. If you open up accounts with Victoria's Secret and Nordstrom on the same day, it will be obvious to creditors and credit reporting agencies that you are just looking for more credit, and they will penalize you for that.

The fifth and last piece of advice is look at your credit report annually. Scan it carefully for errors. Occasionally things you have paid off won't be taken off your credit report and will continue to negatively affect your credit score. If you do find errors, make sure to dispute them and have them corrected.

Make a Statement

One of the most important things you can do to empower yourself to take control of your finances is to take stock of what you currently have. I suggest making a personal financial statement to take a hard look at your assets and liabilities. Even though it can be daunting, in the long run, it's a good idea to know what you're working with. Sometimes the truth hurts, but knowledge is power. Get into the habit of updating this statement quarterly. This will come in handy when you're trying to apply for a mortgage or refinance your home. These are all the things a lender is going to want to see, so it's helpful to have them all on hand now so you don't have to track them down later.

> Even though it can be daunting, in the long run, it's a good idea to know what you're working with. Sometimes the truth hurts, but knowledge is power.

With these basics in mind, we can move on to the critical money and life issues that apply directly to you—whether you're building your own empire (chapter 4), investing like a pro (chapter 7), marrying your sweetheart (chapter 5), or prepping for a sweet new addition to your family (chapter 6), I've got you covered. Feel free to hop to the table of contents and select the chapter that best suits your current financial state or read through them all for a helpful blueprint on thriving personally and professionally. Next up is moving up the ladder at work and killing it along the way.

Chapter 2

GET IT, GIRL: CLIMB
THAT LADDER

It's been a handful of years since college and you're starting to make your way in the professional world—cashing checks, taking names, and moving up the ladder. Those rounds upon rounds of coffee runs for the boss, endless errands, and late nights at your desk are starting to pay off. Go you!

Raises and bonuses are finally coming your way, and it might be time to upgrade some aspects of your life. (Hello, gorgeous designer purse. Or even just dinner that isn't ramen!) But before you shell out for that buttery leather tote or make your first reservation at Per Se, let's make sure your money's in order. You've got the basics down, but there are certain considerations to make as you graduate from Money 101 to real-deal #adulting.

Pump Up Your Emergency Fund

Let's start with a friendly reminder to create or bolster your emergency fund with some extra cash. Maybe you didn't make enough to create a comfy cushion when you first started out. I get it—there's only so much to go around and a girl's gotta eat!

But once that cash is reliably coming in, give yourself the gift of peace of mind with an account that can cover life's inevitable surprises. As a reminder, your emergency fund should have enough money for six months of expenses. That way if you lose your job, quit to follow your dreams, or make a big move, you don't have to worry about affording essentials such as health insurance or toilet paper. If your emergency fund can already weather whatever's thrown your way—whether it's a rainy day or a hurricane—great! It's time to move on and think about how you can do more now to set yourself up later in life.

Harness the Power of Compounding Interest

So many people consider retirement to be the endgame, but it's crucial to think about it at the very beginning—all the way until you're silver haired and waving *bon voyage* to your day job. When you're just gaining ground in your career, it's easy to feel like you make too little money to save for retirement. Maybe you assume you'll really start saving when you're finally raking it in—usually not until your late thirties or early forties. You might think that the few extra dollars you have right now aren't worth socking away because they won't amount to much anyway. I'm here to tell you that they do. Every little bit counts, and here's why: *compound interest.*

Even if you're not contributing very much to your retirement account, those dollars add up thanks to the magic of compound interest. Because the money you put into your retirement fund stays in an account—ideally untouched until you hit at least fifty-nine and a half—it's always being reinvested. That means you're making interest, and then you make interest *on that interest.* With compound interest on your side, a little goes a long way. And by the same token, it's very hard to make up for all those years of compounding interest if you don't start saving until late in the game.

Let's take a look at some hypothetical numbers to get a better idea of how this all plays out. Say you start saving $200 per month at twenty-five and keep it up until your retirement party forty years later. You'd have contributed a total of $96,000 over the course of your career, and with a return on investment of about 6 percent, your account would be stocked with $402,492 on day one of retirement as you head for the golf course or your granddaughter's recital.

Meanwhile, if you started saving at thirty-five, contributing the same $200 per month for the next thirty years, you'd have put a total of $72,000 into your account—only $24,000 less. And yet there would be only $203,118 in there on retirement day—about half as much as if you had started ten years earlier![3] No one wants a retirement full of boxed mac and cheese and regrets; you want to be that grandma on the golf course. If you haven't started saving yet, now's the time!

> No one wants a retirement full of boxed mac and cheese and regrets; you want to be that grandma on the golf course. If you haven't started saving yet, now's the time!

Maybe you're making more than when you first started out, but after all your bills are paid, there isn't a lot left over to put toward retirement. That's okay! Contribute what you can. I promise it will be worth it. But here's the thing: don't just set it and forget it.

Beef Up Your Retirement Contributions

Most people put less than 6 percent into their retirement account, and while doing something is definitely better than nothing, unfortunately, it's not enough long term. You'll likely need about ten times your preretirement income to keep you comfortable through your golden years, and that requires saving more of your earnings as soon as you're able to.

---

3   Kiersz, "Here's the Difference between Someone Who Starts Saving at 25 vs. Someone Who Starts Saving at 35," *Business Insider*, March 25, 2014, https://www.businessinsider.com/saving-at-25-vs-saving-at-35-2014-3.

As you start making more money, you'll have more to work with—and while you can and should treat yourself a bit more (check out chapter 8 for some great options on how to invest in self-care), you should be saving more too.

Making tweaks to your retirement account as your income goes up is super important and will pay off big time later. When those raises and bonuses start coming in, remember to check on your 401(k) and bump up your contributions accordingly.

If you're out of your twenties and just starting to save, I would recommend playing with a retirement calculator to determine how much to sock away. A calculator will allow you to put in different contribution amounts and see how much you'll end up with at retirement age. That way, you can set expectations and manage your budget accordingly. You can find a great retirement calculator on my website, ArianaMangum.com.

Don't Forget Your HSA

This is a great time to make sure you're putting enough in your health or flexible savings account, those tax-advantaged heroes that let you set aside money for health-related expenses. I can't overstate how huge these can be when it comes to saving you cash, letting you buy everything from prescriptions and copays to contact lenses and sunscreen with pretax dollars. Flip back to chapter 1 for more information on the many benefits of HSAs and FSAs and how to use yours to the fullest.

Invest in Employee Stock Options

If you work for a large company and you're headed up the ladder—moving into management or even the C-suite, you may be looking at a new incentive to do well: stock options. Employee stock options offer the holder the right to buy company stock at a specified price.

Usually, you'll get a set amount of stock options, but you'll have to wait a period of time, often a year or so, in order to actually exercise them—or purchase options at the price you've been offered. This is called a vesting period. Delayed gratification, in the form of stock options, is your company's way of encouraging you to do your part to drive the stock price up. Since you have a real stake in it and the option to get those shares at a lower price, it behooves you to help the company soar.

Here's an example to help clarify how stock options work. Let's say your company's stock is trading at $100, but the stock option they're giving you allows you to buy it at $50. Once it's vested, you can purchase shares for $50 a pop and do one of two things: you can hold the stock and wait for the share price to go up or sell it at $100 and make a cool $50 profit per share (well, slightly less—but we'll get to that in a second).

But there's also an expiration date on that offer. They might only give you a month or three to make your purchase. If that period passes before you buy, sorry, you're out of luck. That's why it's important to know the ins and outs of your company's plan and its terms. There are a few different types of employee stock options out there; we'll break them down below.

NONQUALIFIED STOCK OPTIONS AND INCENTIVE STOCK OPTIONS

There are two primary types of stock options: nonqualified stock options (NSOs) and incentive stock options (ISOs). With a non-qualified stock option, you don't pay to hold the shares up front, but as soon as you exercise them, tax comes into play. In addition, if you sell them as soon as you can—when the vesting period is up—it will be considered a short-term capital gain, and you'll pay ordinary income tax on them. If you decide to hold them for two years or longer, you'll pay long-term capital gains, which have a reduced rate. Depending on your income, those long-term earnings are taxed at just 0 to 20 percent, so it probably pays to hold out if you can.

ISOs are usually reserved for upper-level management or executives and get better tax benefits than any other type of employee stock option plan. Federal income tax doesn't factor in when you exercise them, and after two years from the grant date, any gains or losses are considered long term, meaning better tax rates for you.

With both of these options, one of the biggest mistakes people make is selling too soon. That two-year mark necessary to avoid paying short-term gains begins when you are granted the options. If you are granted the options in 2018 and you can't actually exercise them until 2019, you have to hold them until 2020 to make it into long-term territory.

PHANTOM STOCK PLANS

These are referred to as phantom or shadow plans because the stocks in them don't actually exist. With phantom stock plans, some employees—often members of the senior management team—are granted the benefits of stock ownership without actually receiving shares. Even though the physical shares don't exist, the phantom stock behaves just like actual shares would, and employees are paid out any profits that the stock makes.

Stock Appreciation Rights

Stock appreciation rights, or SARs, also fall under the phantom stock umbrella. These are basically incentives to increase a company's value. Rather than giving you stock outright, your employer may say that if their stock does well, you will get some direct benefits. The idea is that if you help boost the value of the company's shares, you'll benefit directly, though it may be in the form of a cash bonus—not stock itself.

EMPLOYEE STOCK OWNERSHIP PLANS

With employee stock ownership plans, you receive shares of company stock at no cost to be held in a plan until you retire or leave the company, at which point the company buys them back. And—bonus—you're only taxed when you sell them, making these plans a particular win.

Usually at the end of the year, companies will give you a window where you can buy stock at a price below market value. When that happens, it might be a good idea to put more of your portfolio into company stock since you'll be able to get a good deal.

THINK BEFORE YOU BUY

While employee stock options may sound great (and they can be!), there are some things to think about when you're considering how much to invest in company stock. While it's a major boon to be able to buy stock at $50 per share, a year from now if its value appreciates, if it remains stagnant, or drops to $48 per share, you essentially make zero. While that certainly doesn't mean you should disregard stock options, there is the chance that you won't get as much as you might think. If you're mostly counting on these funds to cover retirement costs and the share price plummets or the company implodes, you could end up in big trouble.

That's why diversity is essential when it comes to your financial future. Employee stock options are an important part of the game, but they're just one player in a team of talented (and diverse) ballers, and it's crucial to keep that in mind as you think about strategy. For more insight on how to get your portfolio in shape, check out chapter 7, "Financial DIY."

You're totally killing it at work, and with a few simple tweaks to make sure your money's growing alongside your career, you'll have life pretty much handled too. You'll also be ready to tackle the next phase, whatever that may be. And no matter where you're headed right now, I've got tips for you. Now we'll cover something we can all benefit from: little ways to save big.

Chapter 3

SO YOU'RE A FRUGAL BITCH (AND IF YOU'RE NOT, YOU WILL BE SOON!)

hether you're dominating financially or counting down the days until you're no longer haunted by student loans or a subpar salary, we could all benefit from saving a bit more.

Older people tell us all the time that the way to do that is to eliminate small indulgences. "If you would just cut out your daily latte," they say, "you'd save about a thousand dollars a year!" Or "Maybe if you didn't love avocado toast so much, you'd have a house by now!"

That irks me to no end. Maybe in their generation, brewing coffee at home was the thing to do, but to me, Starbucks is a cult— in the best possible way. That feeling of walking through those doors, knowing the muted tones, plush chairs, and soft soundtrack will be there to welcome me whether I'm in Los Angeles, Nashville, or Shanghai, is a remarkable feeling. Ordering my drink just how I like it and sipping it quietly during my commute before entering the chaos of a Tuesday is often just what I need to get out there and slay the day.

If the idea of ditching your beloved pumpkin spice latte or weekly manicure fills you with dread, don't fret! The next time someone starts telling you about the myriad benefits of making coffee at home or painting your own nails, just nod politely, knowing there are tons of little ways to save without giving up the pleasures that make the world more bearable.

In this chapter, we'll cover some cool tricks that can help you save for the things you want without sacrificing your favorite treats.

While none of them will be a windfall, they can help you afford your habits or save toward bigger goals, like eventually buying that Louis Vuitton you've been eyeing, paying for a dream wedding, or even locking down the keys to a new house. Just as it's up to you to choose how to spend your cash, you can also pick the saving tips that fit your lifestyle best. Think of this as a choose-your-own-adventure approach to your wallet. And hopefully, with that comes some free peace of mind.

> Just as it's up to you to choose how to spend your cash, you can also pick the saving tips that fit your lifestyle best.

Ready? Great. Feel free to grab a twelve-dollar slice of avocado toast and settle in.

Make the Most of Your Tax Deductions

One great way to save is to lower the amount of taxes you're responsible for. When you have to pay less, you obviously get to keep more. With some planning, you can deduct some everyday costs and keep more of your hard-earned check. Here are some things you can write off with just a little extra work:

SAVE MORE WHEN YOU BUY A CAR

Typically, when you buy a car, you finance it—and that means there's an interest rate involved. Unfortunately, the interest on that payment is not tax deductible. But it could be. If you have a home, you can use it to help you pay less and get more back. Instead of taking out a car loan, you could take out a home equity loan. Boom! That interest is now tax deductible. And better yet, home equity loans often come with lower interest rates, meaning you save even more. While we're not talking about megabucks here, it could mean adding a pedicure into the rotation every now and then.

BE SMART WITH CREDIT CARDS

In an ideal world, everyone would treat credit cards like checks or debit cards, only using them to pay for things they already have the cash to cover. But for many people, that's pretty unrealistic. If you can't pay off your whole credit card bill every month—and you have a home—you can also use a home equity line of credit to make those monthly payments a little lighter. Simply attach your card to a home equity line of credit, watch that interest rate drop, and write it off at the end of the year. Poof—a few simple tweaks and you're paying less.

USE THAT HSA!

I've said it once (well, more than once), and I'll say it again: use that HSA! Everything you put in that account is pretax money, making those copays, prescriptions, and tons of other everyday items automatically cheaper. What are you waiting for? Do it now—I'll wait!

BUYING A HOUSE BEFORE
MARRIAGE? MAKE YOUR LONG-TERM
RELATIONSHIP WORK FOR YOU

Maybe you've been with your boo for what feels like forever, but for whatever reason, marriage just isn't in the cards at the moment.

If you're currently shacking up and thinking about investing in a home—or you already own one together—you can get twice the tax benefit.

As long as you're both on the loan, each of you can deduct all the interest you're paying. If just one of you is taking the deduction, you're giving the government money that's rightfully yours. Just think about what you could do with that extra cash!

KEEP YOUR DOCTOR BUT DROP THE TRAVEL EXPENSE

You've been going to the same doctor forever. You really like her, and she knows the ins and outs of your medical history. Unfortunately, you just found out you're moving. The good news is if you want to keep seeing her, you don't have to absorb the extra cost to get there! Since she has special knowledge of your medical history, you have the right to deduct the travel expenses necessary to see her. As of this writing, the deduction for miles driven is 0.58/mile, and if you have to fly, yes, that is deductible too.

GET INFORMED ABOUT YOUR HEALTH ON UNCLE SAM'S DIME

Let's say you develop a gluten intolerance, and you don't even know where to start. You've been eating gluten your whole life, and now you're finding out that there's gluten in all kinds of random things— soy sauce, ketchup, beer. If you were to go to a conference to learn about gluten intolerance, all the corresponding expenses—travel, hotel, food, and more—are tax deductible. The same goes for learning about a condition affecting a parent or loved one.

DEDUCT THE COST OF A MORE NUTRITIOUS LIFESTYLE

If a nutritionist or doctor puts you on a weight-loss program or detox to manage a condition such as Crohn's disease, you may be able to write off part of that lifestyle shift. If you have to spend more money than you normally would on food, you can deduct the difference. So fill that Whole Foods cart with confidence, knowing you won't have to eat the extra cost.

Shop and Sell Smart

In addition to saving on your tax bill, there are tons of ways to save by shopping smarter—and actually *make* money on the stuff you don't want anymore. Usually, all it takes is a little time and creativity to make your typical habits work for you.

KNOW WHEN ONLINE IS THE WAY TO GO

According to ConsumerReports.org, there are a number of products that are almost always cheaper online. Electronics, small appliances, pet supplies, theme park tickets, and—a big one—baby supplies are all worth buying on the internet.[4] Rather than running to the supermarket or pharmacy for that box of Huggies, plan ahead and order online for a deep discount.

Amazon's Subscribe and Save program is an excellent example of a way to do this. Toilet paper, paper towels, toothpaste, contact solution, anything I use on a daily basis, I look for on Amazon. Why?

---

4   "When It Really Pays to Buy Online: How to Know Whether You're Better Off Shopping Digitally or in a Store," *Consumer Reports*, May 28, 2015, https://www.consumerreports.org/cro/magazine/2015/05/when-it-really-pays-to-buy-online/index.htm.

Products on Amazon are usually cheaper to begin with, and when you set up a subscription, you save even more.

What's better, if you subscribe to five items, you save 5 percent. When you subscribe to seven or more, your savings go up to 15 percent! Subscribe and Save pays off any way you slice it—not to mention the benefit of not having to worry about running out of the essentials.

MAKE ONLINE SHOPPING EVEN BETTER

I love shopping online. If I know exactly what I want—for instance, Lululemon's Wunder Under yoga pants—and I know my size, there's no reason for me to go into the store. I can be in my pajamas, cozied up in bed, clicking my way to spandex bliss. One thing that makes it even better? Rakuten.com, formally known as Ebates.

Simply go to the site and sign up with your basic information. Once it's installed, all you do is shop like you normally do online and get 1 to 40 percent cash back on brands you love. Once you buy, the money you save goes directly into a PayPal account, accumulating dollars you never would have had otherwise.

If a store is offering a particular discount, Rakuten lets you know with a little pop-up box. For instance, I'd been coveting a certain Burberry scarf forever, but I'd never seen anything Burberry on sale. Neiman Marcus sells Burberry, and at one point, the department store was offering 12 percent cash back on purchases through Rakuten. I bought the scarf, and that 12 percent was all mine.

If you're going to spend the money anyway, let Rakuten tell you if cash back could be in the cards for you. Even better, if the item you want is sold at a few different stores, you can hop on Rakuten's site and see if any of them are offering a deal—and pick the best one if there are multiple shops to choose from.

SELL YOUR STUFF

We've all heard about making extra cash by selling clothes we don't wear anymore, but it always seemed like too much of a hassle for me. That is, until one fateful day.

I had the weekend to myself, and I was cleaning out my closet. Months earlier, I had been on a kick for Teekis—yoga pants covered in crazy prints that were cool for a hot second. When they came out, I bought them in droves but didn't consider the fact that finding a top that didn't clash would be nearly impossible. I ended up wearing them a couple of times before tucking them away for good.

When I happened upon the stack in my closet, I thought about donating them, but they were pretty much brand new, and I had paid almost $100 a pair! I decided it was worth a shot to sell them online. I downloaded Vinted, an app that lets you upload pictures and sell your stuff for free. After snapping a couple of shots, I put them up at a 50 percent discount. Then I forgot about them. A week or two later, someone bought four pairs. For just a few snapshots and mere minutes of my time, I had made $200.

While Vinted is great for everyday stuff—brands such as Nike, Levi's, Gap, and Ugg—there are also sites that specialize in higher-end items. If you have some luxury goods that are still in great shape but not quite your style anymore, you can send them off to a good home and make some cash in the process. Sites such as Poshmark and the RealReal are great for these types of items.

Work Your Credit, Rewards, and Apps

Once you've got your shopping and selling strategies down, there are plenty of other hacks you can implement to help you save every day.

Tapping into credit card benefits, rewards programs, and money-saving apps can help you pinch pennies painlessly and keep more in your pocket. Here are some tips to help you work with every tool available to you.

Tapping into credit card benefits, rewards programs, and money-saving apps can help you pinch pennies painlessly and keep more in your pocket.

GET A NEW CARD

If you don't have too many credit cards and you're thinking about making a big purchase, shop around and see if there are any with great introductory offers—especially when you spend a lot in the first month. For instance, signing up for a new card that gives you megamiles when you register, and zero interest for the first year, might be the perfect tool to cover a new washer and dryer.

ASK AND YOU SHALL RECEIVE

Let's say you've already got enough cards, but you still need to make a big purchase—and you know you're not going to be able to pay it off at the end of the month. You can still get some of those new card perks. All you have to do is ask. Give the company a call, let them know you're buying something big, and ask if you can get a break on the interest for a year. Most of the time, if your request is reasonable, they'll accommodate you.

Don't be afraid to ask for discounts elsewhere too. When you're managing your cable and phone bills, signing up for new services, or working with a vendor, just go for it. You won't believe how willing people are to help you if you just put it out there. Plus, the worst thing they can do is say no.

SIGN UP FOR REWARDS

Tons of places offer rewards just for shopping there, and they can really pay off. If you don't take advantage of these free programs, you'll be missing out. I learned this the hard way. I often book flights for my husband and myself on Southwest Airlines because the prices are great. They offer a rewards program that doesn't require a credit card, and when they sent me the sign-up online, I thought, *Why not?* But I didn't register my husband. I figured the kickback would be small anyway, and it wouldn't be worth the time to set up a separate account.

For the next three years, I booked flights on the airline, paying little to no mind to the rewards. When I got an email out of the blue suggesting I check them out, I clicked over to their site, expecting to see just a handful of points. But in my account was $500!

It dawned on me that if I had signed my husband up, we'd have double that—enough to fund a fun getaway or two for free! From that day forward, I vowed never to skip out on a rewards program, no matter how insignificant it seemed. Whether it's your local pharmacy, grocery store, stylist, or coffee shop, sign up and get that free stuff!

GET RID OF SUBSCRIPTIONS YOU DON'T USE

It's easy to sign up for a membership and totally forget about it—especially if the cost is small. Months or even years later, when you realize you haven't used it at all, those fees are still coming out of your account on the regular. And like anything, those subscriptions add up. You may realize you have four streaming accounts and only use one or that iTunes is docking you $20 per month for music you're not even listening to. With a quick scan of your credit cards and checking account, you can save hundreds of dollars a year by eliminating subscriptions you don't use.

INVEST YOUR CHANGE

If you ever saved up for a Barbie or a bike as a kid by dropping coins into a piggy bank, you know firsthand that every little bit helps. Back in the day, banks embraced a similar system, letting you sign up for a program where every purchase you made would be rounded up to the next dollar. The difference would then be deposited into a savings account. Over time, those pennies would add up.

Today, thanks to technology, the 2.0 version of systems like these have arrived. There are apps that allow you to save in the same way, rounding up your purchases to the next dollar and plopping that extra change into a separate account. And now, with an app called Acorns, you can make that money grow. Acorns takes your extra change and invests it. That means you get a return in addition to whatever you're putting away.

The best part of systems like these is that you don't even feel the pinch! I guarantee you're not thinking about the extra $0.25 from your $3.75 morning latte, and yet it's working for you. One thing to note: since your change is being invested, you are subject to losses, just like any other investment in the market. So there could be instances where you end up with less than what you put in.

DON'T SLEEP ON DIGIT

Another name to remember in the app world? Digit. Most of us have heard about sinking funds—putting away a small amount of money each month to save for a larger purchase. People typically use this technique to save for big events such as Christmas and vacations. It's pretty easy to stash $50 per month. If you start at the beginning of the year, come Christmas, you'll have $550 to spend on friends and loved ones.

Digit makes this even easier! You simply link it to your checking account, and it analyzes your spending habits and your income. Based on its findings, it deducts a smaller amount of money as often as every day, or larger amounts when it knows you're expected to have income, and moves it into a savings account for you. It also offers a host of other great features. For only $2.99 a month, you get a 1 percent savings bonus every three months. You can also add multiple savings goals to your account, and Digit will divide the money among them. For example, you could be saving toward Christmas, your student loan, a vacation, and a down payment on a new home all at once. You can "boost" certain goals so some save more than others at a faster rate, and you can pause savings on any goal for however long you'd like at any time. You can also set it up to transfer money back into your checking account—and/or stop saving altogether—if your balance gets below an amount you set, and you can set a maximum savings amount per day for each goal you have. And if the app happens to take too much from your account and you incur an overdraft penalty, Digit will cover the fee!

SWITCH YOUR BANK

We all get notices in the mail from banks offering special deals and cold, hard cash when you sign up for an account. Switching up your bank, and getting some free money in the process, could be a good way to make a quick buck here and there.

The Bottom Line: Find Money-Saving Tips That Work for You

There are a million and one ways to save a little more. You can use the ones here to get started, but there are tons of sites out there dedicated to providing information about keeping—and growing—your cash in innovative ways. During your downtime, you can search Google or Pinterest for extra insights that can help you make little changes that work for you. I guarantee you'll feel pretty proud when you've built up a little nest egg without really thinking about it.

The secret to saving successfully and staying happy during the process is doing it on your terms. Choose the methods that work for you. Don't cut out the small luxuries that keep you going just because someone tells you to. When it comes to odd ways to save, you can have your latte and drink it too!

Chapter 4

TAPPING INTO YOUR INNER #GIRLBOSS: KILLING IT AS AN ENTREPRENEUR

$\mathcal{H}$ ave you ever dreamed about opening your own shop full of the coolest indie brands or fantasized about turning your side hustle making artisanal jams into a full-time gig? Today's entrepreneurial culture and a wealth of free and easy-to-use online resources make running your own business more accessible than ever. If you've got a great idea and the drive, you can make it happen.

Perhaps you have already launched your own business, and you're ready to take your venture—and your life—to the next level, but you're not sure about next steps. In this chapter, we'll cover crucial personal and professional strategies, tips, and tricks to keep in mind when you're becoming your very own #GirlBoss.

Becoming a Bona Fide Business

When you're ready to become a real-deal business, there are a few steps you need to take to make it all official. First, you'll need a business license to operate in your city. Head to your local city hall to apply for one.

Next, if you're going to be buying goods wholesale—say, cute tees from your favorite small designer or fresh blooms for your budding floral business—you'll need to apply to your state's board of equalization for your seller's permit. This is pretty crucial because anytime you make a purchase, the wholesaler is going to ask for this document. Have it on hand before you start calling vendors, and they'll know you have your stuff together.

And if you're selling material goods—whether it's a hobby or your sole income—consider doing so through an established vendor site such as Etsy to help make life easier. If you earn more than $600, they'll send you a 1099 at tax time, showing exactly how much money you made. When all your income is automatically documented, you don't have to worry about making math mistakes or forgetting to log a purchase.

The Benefits of Being Women Owned

There are also some awesome perks for women who have majority ownership of their businesses. On the US Small Business Administration's website, SBA.gov, you can find a ton of links with information and opportunities specifically for women-owned businesses. Information is categorized by the type of business you're opening, and benefits include access to loans, better rates, credit, federal contracts, counseling, and business training.

In addition to tools and information specifically for women, the federal government aims to award at least 5 percent of all their contracts to women-owned businesses, so you might want to consider bringing on the government as a key client![5] As long as you're at least 51 percent owned and controlled by women, you're eligible. You can easily get certified as a women-owned small business on the US Small Business Administration's website and compete for these valuable contracts.

---

5   "Women-Owned Small Business Federal Contracting Program," SBA.gov, US Small Business Administration, June 5, 2018.

The Beauty of QuickBooks

Once you're up and running, having a tool to organize your accounting is essential. You want to make sure that you're tracking all your expenses, invoices, and payments and keeping them separate from your personal accounts. A program such as QuickBooks is an excellent way to put everything in order.

At the beginning, it's easy to put purchases on your credit or debit card—especially if your business is too new to provide you with credit. If you do so, use one credit card solely for business expenses, and set up a separate checking account as well. This will help you stay organized and keep your business expenses well defined so you're not trying to track down the information when it's time to do your taxes. It will also save you a ton of money because your accountant won't have to spend time—and billable hours—sorting everything out at the end of the year.

My husband and I learned this the hard way. When we started Miramontes Capital, we were commingling all our expenses—using the same credit and debit cards for business and personal purchases alike. At the end of the year, our records were a mess. Our accountant was able to bail us out, but the cost was exorbitant because he had to go through every single transaction—something we could've been doing on our own from the start.

Worse, if you get audited and you don't have receipts, you're in big trouble. This too happened to us! We got audited our first year in business and were required to produce all our receipts and all our invoices. Because we hadn't yet gotten on track with QuickBooks, it was a huge hassle. Not only did we have to pay our accountant to go back and look through everything for the year, we also had to call all our vendors and try to get receipts. Save yourself the hassle and anxiety and do it from day one.

If you're not sure how to set up QuickBooks, no worries—you can always bring in help. You don't have to hire a full-time employee to figure it out (and besides, that may not be in your budget as a new business owner). There are many companies out there that take on tasks such as this one, and because you're just paying for what you need, their assistance is affordable. You can either hire them to set up the program and teach you how to enter expenses yourself in a single session, or you can pay them to monitor your account and record transactions on an ongoing basis.

I went with the former option, and today, it takes me about twenty minutes a week to enter all our transactions and pay invoices. However, since I'm not a chief financial officer or an accountant, I outsource our monthly financial reporting and pay an expert to provide a big picture view of what's happening moneywise. You can assess your situation and determine the balance that works for you.

Take Advantage of Taxes

Another benefit of tracking your expenses is tax write-offs. Normally, when you pay for your home, your car, or your lunch, you cover those items with after-tax dollars. But if you're using them for your enterprise, you can write them off—essentially telling the IRS that they are business expenses and therefore shouldn't count toward any distributions you're taking—and ultimately lower your tax bill. Here are just a few of the things you can write off as a business owner:

- A portion of your rent or mortgage payment. If you work from home, you can deduct a portion of your rent or mortgage payment, as that money would otherwise go toward renting office space—a business expense.

- Car payments or the cost of gas. If your business requires you to do a lot of driving, you can deduct part of your payments toward your car or gas to help lighten the burden.

- The cost of entertaining clients. Let's say you have a lot of lunch meetings, throw parties to help cultivate customers, or offer seminars at restaurants. You can write off half of that and put those savings toward your own dining adventures.

HARNESS THE HOBBY PROVISION

Even if you're not quite ready to fully commit to your venture, you can still tap into a wealth of tax benefits. While you can't take a loss on a hobby like you can a business, you can utilize the hobby provision and take some sweet—and potentially significant— deductions. Materials, supplies, and any miles that you drive in service of your hobby can all be deducted from your income, as can a portion of your rent or mortgage, utility bills, and homeowners' or renters' insurance. These costs may seem small, but they can definitely add up. And with those savings, you may even be able to invest more in your fledgling business, inching your way closer to living the dream full time.

Payroll, Healthcare, and Retirement Savings

Whether you're a one-woman shop or you've got an office full of employees, payroll, healthcare, and retirement savings are all essential considerations. Your approach will differ depending on whether you're on your own or responsible for others, so let's discuss.

IF YOU'RE FLYING SOLO

When you're working for someone else, taxes are taken out of each paycheck, and at the end of the year, your company provides you with a W-2 that sums it all up. But as a business owner, it's on you to determine your tax accountability.

If you're on your own, things are still pretty simple. Just know that you're going to be responsible for paying taxes on everything you earn, and when you transfer money from your business's checking account to your personal one, think about what you'll owe. Each time you take a distribution, deduct funds for taxes and either pay them to the IRS and your state immediately, or set them aside in a savings account so you know you'll have the funds at the end of the year. You may even want to speak with your certified public accountant (CPA) because estimated tax payments may be required. This is where you make quarterly tax payments based on your expected income.

> Whether you're a one-woman shop or you've got an office full of employees, payroll, healthcare, and retirement savings are all essential considerations.

Without a formal employer, you'll also need to choose your own healthcare plan. You can either shop for plans yourself or hire an expert—a healthcare broker—to assess your needs and advise you on the best options available.

And don't forget: saving for retirement is still crucial when you're working for yourself. You can—and should—contribute to a retirement plan, such as a self-employed 401(k). This type of plan has a $55,000 maximum contribution annually, and once you hit age fifty, you can add an additional $18,500 in salary deferrals each year. Keep in mind that with any retirement-saving vehicle you cannot pull the money out until you're fifty-nine and a half without incurring a penalty. Moreover, these limits can change yearly, so pop on Google and check for the current year's contribution limits.

IF YOU'RE LEADING A TEAM

Once you bring on employees, there's a lot more to think about. You're not just responsible for your own livelihood anymore, and you have to plan accordingly. There's payroll, healthcare, and human resources (HR) to consider in addition to helping your team save for retirement. Can you handle it all on your own?

Sure. You can search for health companies, set up QuickBooks to do your payroll, and process those checks bimonthly. You can be HR and manage all that—including staying up to date on current employment laws and making sure you're in compliance.

But when you take on every task, you'll soon find yourself being stretched, and it won't be in the direction you want. Maybe you went into business because you loved making jewelry or grooming dogs or home organizing, but now you're spending time on other components of your company, stuff that just pulls you away from the heart of your business.

This is where a professional employer organization, or PEO, comes in. These companies can take over all the tasks that distract you from your passion. They can do payroll processing, HR management, benefits administration, insurance plans, COBRA (the Consolidated Omnibus Budget Reconciliation Act), workers' compensation, safety programs, retirement plans—you name it. And when you're part of a PEO, healthcare and retirement plan rates are lower since you're part of a large pool of companies accessing their services. This can help a lot if you're contributing toward those costs for employees. PEOs can also keep you up to date on compliance for employment laws and provide any necessary signage, which is essential if you don't want to incur a hefty fine.

As with anything, there are some cons to a PEO, and one is cost. Every PEO has a different cost structure and different offerings. For example, some may have steeper rates because they provide a more robust HR service, something you may not require if you only have a handful of employees. It's important to choose a provider that matches your needs, so take the time to search for the right plan. For my business, I have found a PEO extremely helpful, especially when it comes to changing employment laws. They keep me up to date on the current laws and let me know when changes need to occur to keep me compliant. Employment lawsuits are no joke, so when it comes to making sure everything is buttoned up and in compliance, the cost is well worth it for my business.

FUND THE FUTURE

When choosing retirement plans, you can go through your PEO, opting for the one they offer, but after weighing the costs and benefits, you may want to set up your own.

There are three options here:

1. a 401(k),

2. an SEP IRA, and

3. a simple IRA.

Here are the perks and pitfalls of each.

401(k)

For a small business, 401(k) plans are often expensive because of all the administration involved. I wouldn't recommend them unless you're gaining access to one through a PEO that mitigates some of the cost.

If you do choose to use a PEO-sponsored 401(k), there is one thing to consider. For all 401(k) plans, discrimination testing must be done once a year. It's a tedious and time-consuming process, requiring that all employees be surveyed. However, if you match 4 percent of every employee's contribution, you can forego the testing process. You may decide that it's worth it to choose the 401(k) and match at 4 percent to keep things simple.

SEP IRA

SEPs are for self-employed people or small business owners. As with a traditional IRA, funds are taxed upon withdrawal. Only employers can contribute to SEP IRAs. As of 2018, you can pay up to 25 percent of compensation, or $55,000 per year, whichever is less. If you want to fully fund your employees' retirement, this may be an option worth looking into, but if they're going to be investing as well, this is not the plan for you.

Simple IRA

Simple IRAs are only available to businesses with one hundred or fewer employees. Both employers and employees can contribute, but employers must match 3 percent of employees' salaries. The maximum contribution on this type of account is $12,500 per year, and the catch-up at age fifty is $3,000 per year—the lowest maximum contribution rate out of all the plans discussed here. If you want to give your team the opportunity to save as much as possible, this may not be the right choice.

Hire Help

Unsure if you need employees in the first place? Maybe you're just testing the waters and all these expenses seem totally overwhelming, but you're putting in twenty-hour days and you know you need extra hands, like, yesterday. If you're not exactly sure how many people you might need as you get your business off the ground or to the next level (and how to afford the corresponding expenses), but you know you need help, consider hiring a W-9 employee.

With W-9 employees, you simply fill out tax form W-9, have them sign it, and pay them for the work they complete. You'll record all the payments you make to them throughout the year and have your accountant send them a 1099. That's where your responsibility ends. You don't have to provide insurance, and you don't have to withhold taxes from their earnings—all that's on them. From there, you can evaluate whether full-time assistance would be worth your while.

Dress for Success

While you're getting into the nitty-gritty of business operations, don't forget about yourself. You've most definitely heard that you should dress for the job you want, and I wholeheartedly endorse that adage. The way you look has a tremendous impact on how you feel, and if you feel like you're going to kill it, you will.

When you put the time and energy into looking your best, others will take note as well. They'll have more confidence in your ability to do whatever you do best. Whether that means you slip into an amazing business suit that makes you feel like C-suite material or tie on a chic apron that says, "I'm a celebrity-quality chef," make sure your wardrobe reflects your aspirations.

Surround Yourself with the Best

Once you begin to hit your stride, it's also time to reevaluate your surroundings. When you're just starting out, it's easy to go with the flow. For instance, when I was eighteen, I took the first credit card I was offered—I didn't shop around. The same went for finding a doctor and even friends; for a long time my circle consisted of people I had met in high school.

This is often true when you're starting a business too. We find ourselves picking the most accessible—and often the cheapest—options to keep things moving. But once you have some success, get yourself the best. Here are a few categories to upgrade as you progress.

Your credit cards

A great credit card has significant benefits that can help you grow your business or enjoy your time off. With a little more credit history under your belt, you can search for credit cards with the best rates, as well as rewards that fit your preferences in the form of cash back, travel benefits, or unique experiences.

Your tax professional

Almost anyone can handle taxes when they're just working with a W-2. But as your start-up picks up speed and things get a bit more complicated, you should consider looking for a highly qualified CPA instead of crunching the numbers yourself or letting H&R Block handle things. Whereas the person you meet with at your local tax chain probably took a short course to earn their chair—one they might occupy only during tax season—a CPA has a degree, a license to practice, and documented experience. They can help you employ tax strategies that will save you big time.

Your physician

Maybe you've been seeing the same pediatrician since you were born or you chose your current doctor based on their proximity to your place. Perhaps you depend on your local urgent care office for same-day services when you get sick—even though it wastes an entire afternoon. When things are crazy busy, it can be hard to find the time to research someone new.

- Concierge medical services provide a fantastic option. For a monthly fee, you can text, call, or FaceTime your doctor anytime you need them. They can review your symptoms and call in a prescription on the spot—all while you're at home or in your office. It doesn't get any easier than that. Depending on your insurance, this service may already be offered. For example, my insurance carrier has an app that I can log on to and state what my issue is. Then a doctor calls me within minutes.

Your investments

With a little extra cash flow coming in, this is a good time to diversify your investments. Consider investing in real estate if you don't want to put all your money in the stock market, and find a great agent to help you navigate your options.

Your professional support system

You may have gotten to a great place on your own, but when you're looking to solve a problem or get to the next stage, getting additional support is a great idea. Find a business or life coach who can keep you accountable and give you that extra push; seeking out experts can help you find motivation or generate new insights.

- For example, when I was struggling to create the culture I wanted within my company. I brought in a coach with more than twenty years of management experience to help me achieve my vision. For three months, we talked every week. We bounced ideas off each other, and she shared her thoughts on what was working well and how we could improve the things that weren't. In the end, we were able to build a culture that I'm proud of—one that keeps our team and our clients happy.

Your friends

Your inner circle and their choices and paths often affect your own, so take a good look at your friendships. Are the people you keep closest helping to build you up and make you a stronger, better person, or are they holding you back with petty drama and their own lack of ambition? If it seems like more of the latter is happening, it may be time to look for a new group.

- I struggled with this myself. In college, I had a best friend. We were inseparable. Our endless hangouts and late-night partying worked for us because we had the extra time. But when I graduated and got on with my career, she did not. She was taking a long time to finish school, and accordingly, she was stuck in college mode.

- Soon, I found that our interests and schedules no longer aligned, so I began looking for other connections, women with similar aspirations and ideals—those who were community minded and career driven. Making new connections helped me expand my network in the right direction and introduced me to people and ideas I never would have encountered had I stuck with my college buddy alone.

Your self-care

To get this far, you may have neglected yourself a bit. As you know, the hustle is hard work, and the time and energy you have to spend on yourself is often the first thing to be sacrificed. But you can't keep grinding forever. I know because I've tried.

- I reached a point where things were going well, but they never seemed quite good enough. I became obsessed with getting to the next level as fast as possible. I dedicated every moment of my day to getting better, being smarter, and making more money. I traded in my favorite radio show for audiobooks from successful entrepreneurs and skipped TV entirely to spend more time working. But eventually I couldn't keep it up anymore.

  As you know, the hustle is hard work, and the time and energy you have to spend on yourself is often the first thing to be sacrificed. But you can't keep grinding forever.

- I was crashing and burning, and my anxiety was in full force. I had no choice but to return to my self-care routine. I went back to yoga. I started listening to music again. I let myself have downtime—enough to feel human, enjoy the success I had achieved, and regain the energy to keep moving forward.

- If you've hit pause on your gym routine or left small indulgences such as manicures by the wayside because you've been working 24-7, you need to reinstitute that self-care—especially when you have a little more cash to spend.

Running a business is definitely challenging, but when you put in the time and effort and assemble a strong set of strategies and tools, you'll reach the point when you're ready to share your remarkable product or service with the world—and find serious personal fulfillment in the process. Whether you're just launching your venture or thinking about ways to grow, don't be afraid to trust your instincts, follow your heart, and put in the work. After all, the best possible investment you can make is in yourself.

Chapter 5

HE PUT A RING ON IT: NOW WHAT?

So you're getting married! Congratulations! Along with all the fun stuff planning for a wedding and life together entails, this milestone requires new considerations about how you'll handle your finances going forward. Here are some things to think about after he pops the question.

Get Your Insurance in Order

Imagine this scenario. You get engaged to the man of your dreams. His proposal is amazing: done in front of your closest friends and family at the restaurant where you had your first date, under the fireworks at Cinderella's castle, or on top of a mountain in the Swiss Alps. The ring is perfect, exactly what you'd have chosen for yourself, only better. You get married, go away on this great, white-sand beach honeymoon … and lose your ring in the ocean.

While losing your ring would feel pretty awful under any circumstances, it will feel a whole lot worse if it's not insured and you can't replace it. The first thing you should do when you get engaged—maybe after calling family and friends and racking up some likes on Facebook and Instagram—is insure that gorgeous new bling.

You can easily add it to your renters' or homeowners' policy; just make sure to do it as a line item so you get the exact amount of coverage you need.

Now is also a really great time to make sure the rest of your insurance is in line. If something happens to your spouse, you don't want to be left high and dry—and vice versa.

Whether your future hubby is going to be the primary breadwinner or you're each contributing equally, many of the awesome things you're doing together, such as buying a house or cars and making investments, require at least one income. You want to make sure you can each cover those expenses if—God forbid—something were to happen to one of you. Otherwise, you could be in a tough situation with lots of liabilities and insufficient cash flow.

Life insurance offers valuable coverage and peace of mind. Plus, if you're young and healthy, rates are extremely reasonable. A good rule of thumb is to purchase six to eight times your gross earnings in insurance.

Know before You Go Down the Aisle

It's important to know exactly what you're getting into before you get married, and that means having a (potentially) tough conversation about the assets and debts on both sides of the aisle. You certainly don't want any surprises to come up after saying "I do," so even though it may feel a bit uncomfortable, it's better to get everything out in the open.

During these talks, the topic of a prenuptial agreement may come up. Maybe your soon-to-be husband raises the issue, or maybe you think you might need one. Let's talk about what such an agreement involves so you can be prepared, no matter who suggests it.

A prenuptial agreement, or prenup, covers any assets and debts that each person has before getting married and sets out any financial requirements or conditions that you and your fiancé agree on should your marriage end in divorce. For example, if you're working hard to save for retirement, you may want your prenup to say that in the event of a divorce, you keep everything you've saved—a stipulation that may not otherwise be up to you if you don't have a prenup, depending on your state.

Maybe you own a home or established quite a bit of wealth before you met Mr. Right and you want to protect it going into marriage. Once your assets get commingled, they become community property, and without a prenup spelling out who gets what, you'll probably lose at least part of them in a divorce.

For example, if you bought a home before meeting your fiancé, you may decide that when you get married, your new husband will just move in, and you'll begin making mortgage payments together. If you get divorced ten years later, depending on your state, that home is not considered entirely community assets. The value of your home when you got married would be yours and yours alone, while any growth that occurred during the course of the marriage would be split. Whether or not that seems like a reasonable scenario, a prenup would give you more control over how you want to divide that property and/or its value.

If you determine that you need a prenup, you should each get your own attorney. That way, you have an advocate with your individual priorities in mind, and together you can create a document that benefits both of you.

Choosing Your Castle

Often people start thinking about buying a home around the time they get married. It's exciting to imagine starting your life together in your very own place. But before you start shopping for your dream home, think about whether you're planning to stay put.

If you're not sure where life will take you, it may not be the right time to buy. You don't want to have to sell it the following year if one of you gets a great job offer somewhere else, as it's not likely that home values will have risen enough to sell it for a profit. On top of that, sometimes homes sit on the market for a while, and you don't want to get stuck.

If you're sure you're ready to settle down, we'll get into the ins and outs of what you need to know as you start looking for a home and a mortgage. Luckily, you already have some of the parts of the process in place! Remember the financial statement you created way back in chapter 1? Now is the perfect time to pull it out because when you go to qualify for a loan, the bank or lender is going to ask for all those numbers.

Don't forget about your Mint app either. If you've set it up and had it running in the background, you have a pretty good idea of what you've been spending on a monthly basis and where you've been spending it. With all this great information, you can start thinking about how much income and savings you have available to put toward your new place!

Owning comes with extra costs, so you should factor those into your income and savings as well. Maybe right now your landlord covers things such as maintenance, water, and trash, but soon, all those responsibilities will be yours. Your emergency fund also makes a difference here. Most of the time you don't know that you'll need a new roof in two years or that a pipe is going to burst six months from now, and you'll be grateful for the cushion you've created to absorb those costs.

Prep for Your Down Payment

Know that you'll usually need to put down about 20 percent of your home's price in cash. And don't forget about closing costs—often another 3 percent of the purchase price—which you'll have to pay to cover the appraisal of the property, inspection, issuing of the title, and anything else necessary to finalize the sale. First-time home buyers can get lower rates on the down payment, and there may be specific opportunities available for those within a lower income bracket or with veteran status, so make sure to look into the benefits available to you based on your circumstances.

Tap into the Perks of Prequalification

When you're thinking about buying a home, shopping different banks for loan rates and getting prequalified is a great place to start. The process is usually free through any bank or lender, and it's as easy as contacting your regular bank to find out how much home you can finance.

Prequalification is helpful in a number of ways. First, you know how much you have available to spend, letting you custom tailor your search to homes within your budget. Second, if you find a home you love and you end up in a bidding war, prequalification gives you a leg up. The seller knows you're already approved—and that escrow's going to be a breeze—making you a safer bet than buyers who aren't.

Here's how prequalification works: Your lender will request proof of income and any assets you may have, along with any major out-standing debts—car loans, student loans, and credit card balances. Then the loan officer will pull your credit report. Based on this information, you'll be provided a dollar amount that the lender would feel comfortable providing you along with a projected monthly payment.

A QUICK TIP ON CREDIT

Since lenders will pull your credit information as part of the prequalification process, if you haven't gotten your credit in order yet, hop back to chapter 1 and begin that process. But if you're in a rush and you still need that credit boost—I get it: you're getting married and it would be nice to have a home *now*—you're not out of luck. Here's a great tip to build your credit within ninety days. You just need a relative with a high credit score who would be willing to do you a favor.

All your family member has to do is add you as an authorized user on one of their credit cards. Basically, that relative is just giving you a credit card with your name on it. Now, you don't have to spend anything on the card to have this work, so let your family member know that.

Like magic, within sixty to ninety days, your relative's entire credit history transfers over to you, bumping up your credit score as a result. And luckily for the relative, there is no flip side; your credit score won't affect them at all. With your newly improved credit, you're ready to proceed to prequalification (though you should still work to improve your score on your own).

It doesn't hurt to shop around when you're looking for a lender—do your due diligence and visit at least two or three banks to make sure you're getting the best possible rate.

Pick the Right Mortgage

There are a few types of mortgages to choose from, but the two most popular are fixed-rate and adjustable-rate mortgages.

A fixed-rate mortgage will stay the same no matter what. When you sign on the dotted line, that's your interest rate, and it won't change. Fixed-rate loans are the most popular and almost always the most advisable because they're stable. You know that they're never going to change, so you can budget accordingly.

Adjustable-rate mortgages, as the name suggests, fluctuate. They're usually attractive because the starting rate is lower than a fixed mortgage. People are drawn in by the seemingly low rate, but don't be fooled because these rates can go up yearly, and sometimes the increases make it nearly impossible to make payments from one year to the next.

I learned at a very young age about the impact an adjustable-rate mortgage can have even before I really understood what mortgages meant. My mom and stepdad were married for seventeen years, during which time my stepdad was the breadwinner and took care of all the finances. My mom was basically in the dark—she just relied on him to manage their affairs. But when they decided to get divorced, her lack of knowledge made things difficult.

In the divorce process, my mom got to keep their home. She soon got a job and was making the mortgage payments each month. However, she didn't know that the mortgage had an adjustable rate. From one year to the next, the payment went up by about $1,200 per month. For her, that extra $1,200 was not feasible. And worse, because she hadn't yet built up her own credit history, she couldn't refinance. Ultimately, she had to sell the house and buy something smaller that she could pay mostly cash for.

These kinds of things happen every day. When you don't know what you're dealing with, the outcome is rarely positive. You may get an adjustable-rate mortgage, assuming that by the time the rate goes up, you'll be making more money. Or you may assume that you'll just be able to refinance down the line, but sometimes that's not the case. This is exactly what happened during the housing crisis of 2008, when housing prices dropped so much that refinancing wasn't an option since homes were no longer worth as much as what people had paid for them. Think twice before you sign up for something that will fluctuate—you never know what the circumstances will be like when it does.

> When you don't know what you're dealing with, the outcome is rarely positive.

Interest-only mortgages are technically an option, but you shouldn't even consider them. With these, you're literally *only* paying the interest: you don't even touch the principal. On paper, you've bought a house, but since you're not actually paying any of it back—*ever*—you might as well be renting while calling yourself a homeowner. People are often compelled to take this path because rates appear super low, even lower than an adjustable-rate mortgage. No matter how persuasive those rates appear to be, this is never a good investment.

Fast-Forward: Your Financial Future as Husband and Wife

As you settle down, think about these long-term strategies for a (financially) happy and healthy marriage from honeymoon to first home and all the way through your golden years.

RETIREMENT SAVINGS

As you launch your life together, don't forget about retirement savings. Why?

Have you ever seen those elderly greeters at Walmart? Do you think they're there because they love their work? More likely than not, it's because they didn't save for retirement. A 2018 study by Northwestern Mutual found that one-third of Americans have less than $5,000 saved for retirement, and one in five had no retirement savings *at all*.[6] If you don't consider retirement when you're managing your income now, you're sure to find yourself working long after you'd like to.

Nowadays, in most marriages both spouses work. But even if one of you plans to eventually leave the workforce to raise children or try something creative that won't produce an income for a while, saving for retirement is still important—and you can still contribute.

If you're married and not earning an income, you can make *spousal IRA contributions*. Many people don't know about this option. But with a spousal IRA, you can contribute up to $5,500 per year as of 2018. Over time—say, twenty years or so—this can really go a long way toward maintaining your comfy lifestyle indefinitely.

Here's a great example of how spousal IRA contributions can make all the difference. At Miramontes Capital, 98 percent of our clients are preretirees or retired. I've seen pretty much every scenario possible play out when it comes to saving for retirement—people who have done an excellent job, a mediocre job, or a terrible job over the course of their adult lives.

One of the couples we worked with thought they were doing an excellent job. The wife worked as a bookkeeper early in life and saved about $36,000 toward retirement while she was employed. Then she got pregnant, and the couple decided she would be a stay-at-home mom. Her husband became the sole provider and contributed as much as he could to his 401(k) over the years.

---

6   "1 in 3 Americans Have Less Than $5,000 in Retirement Savings," Northwestern Mutual (news release), May 8, 2018, https://www.prnewswire.com/news-releases/1-in-3-americans-have-less-than-5-000-in-retirement-savings-300643774.html.

During the early years of raising children, he wasn't able to contribute as much—understandable, as kids are quite costly, which you'll see in the next chapter! But later on, he was able to max out his retirement contributions. He could have saved a lot more, but he figured that since he was pouring the maximum amount into that particular account, he would be fine.

When he was about fifty-eight, he started working with us to develop a plan for retirement. We found that he needed another half-million dollars to retire comfortably! All along, he had thought he was on track, but just because you're maxing out your 401(k) doesn't necessarily mean those funds will cover your lifestyle in retirement.

Yet if his wife had taken advantage of the spousal IRA, the couple could have met—or even surpassed—the amount needed to make up the difference.

SOCIAL SECURITY

Say it's been forty years since you first said "I do," and you and your husband live a wonderful life. He has worked continuously for the duration of your relationship. Meanwhile, you were a wage earner in your twenties but stopped to raise your family. Now your husband is about to retire. He has a 401(k), maybe even a pension, and Social Security. Although you contributed through a spousal IRA, you didn't bring in any other income. Does Social Security apply to you? The answer is yes. And better yet, you have options!

Once a year, the Social Security Administration sends out a statement letting you know how much you've paid into the system and what your future benefits might look like. (You can always log on to SSA.gov to access your benefit information as well.) If you didn't work for most of your life, your Social Security benefit may be $600 per month, while your husband's benefit may be $2,200 per month.

When it comes time to collect Social Security, you can choose to take your benefit, *or* you can elect to take half the amount of your spouse's. For example, if your husband's is $2,200, you can receive $1,100 per month. Your choice doesn't affect his benefit at all—he'll still be able to draw his full $2,200.

You can begin taking payments between the ages of sixty-two and sixty-six, but you'll want to be strategic about when you start depending on a number of financial factors. As retirement nears, work with your financial advisor to figure out the optimal age to start collecting.

Although retirement and Social Security checks are a long way off, the more you know about your options, the better you can plan, saving yourself a lot of stress and anxiety. This brings us to some less appealing—but equally important—topics: divorce and death.

Till Divorce or Death Do You Part

You can never predict what will happen in life, so it's important to be as prepared as possible for any circumstances—even those that are upsetting. Divorce and death definitely fall into that category, but if and when you do have to face them, having created a strong plan makes things much easier during an already difficult situation.

KEEP TABS ON YOUR FAMILY'S FINANCIAL INFORMATION

You may be happy to have your spouse handle all the bills and control certain accounts on a daily basis, but it's crucial to have access to all that information just in case you need it. If something terrible happens to your husband—God forbid—or you find yourself in a less-than-amicable divorce, without this knowledge, you're going to be stuck.

Know what your assets are, as well as the accounts you have, where they're housed, whose names are on them, and the log-ins for each one. You should also be aware of the loan information for your home if you have one, including what type of loan you have and whether you're on the title. If anything you find out makes you uncomfortable, talk about it! You don't want to realize too late that you're just an authorized user on your husband's accounts and have to hire an attorney to help claim what's yours, adding even more heartache to an already devastating situation.

Consider Setting Up a Trust

I always recommend that anyone getting married set up a living trust. You can place all your assets into the trust—which you can use and access while you're alive—*and* dictate where those assets go when you die. Having a living trust means you can avoid probate, the lengthy court-driven process of establishing the validity of a will.

If your home and bank accounts are in your trust and something were to happen to you or your husband, the other spouse (or whomever you designate as your beneficiary or beneficiaries) automatically owns your assets. It's a far simpler, shorter process than going through the public court system, which is going to happen without a trust.

You can never predict the future when you get married. You could end up being a stay-at-home mom. You could end up pursuing your own side hustle full time while your husband manages the finances. Maybe you'll stay in love forever and pass away in your sleep holding hands, *Notebook* style. Or things might end more quickly than you ever imagined. Making sure you plan well for your future, and know what you have and where it's located, will help protect you and your family no matter what.

Chapter 6

WHAT TO EXPEND WHEN YOU'RE EXPECTING (AND BEYOND): MANAGING MONEY AS A MOM

*L*ike so many women in their twenties and thirties, you've got babies on the brain. Whether you're just starting to think about expanding your family or you're pregnant right now, you know your life is about to change—big time!

Maybe you've mapped out the basics: you have the perfect name, have picked out the cutest nursery decor, and have read enough parenting books for a second major in swaddling. The next thing to consider may seem a little less sweet: how your new addition will affect your budget.

Besides labor and the incredible responsibility of raising an actual human, the cost of raising a child can be one of the scariest parts of bringing a baby into the world. According to a 2017 report from the US Department of Agriculture, the cost of raising a child born in 2015 through the age of eighteen is approximately $233,610—and that's before factoring in college expenses.[7]

> Besides labor and the incredible responsibility of raising an actual human, the cost of raising a child can be one of the scariest parts of bringing a baby into the world.

Luckily, there are a lot of really great tools that you can use to plan for child-related expenses—especially school savings—so you can spend less time worrying and more time snuggling your little one.

---

7   M. Lino, K. Kuczynski, N. Rodriguez, and T. Schap, "Expenditures on Children by Families, 2015," US Department of Agriculture, Center for Nutrition Policy and Promotion.

Prep for Baby by Building Your Nest Egg

Remember that emergency fund we talked about in chapter 1? That cash really helps here too. With kids, you never know what's going to happen. In addition to all those added expenses—diapers, wipes, tiny outfits they'll immediately outgrow, and the like—they could be born with a disability that requires special care or break their arm or need a mouth full of orthodontia ten years down the line. Building up as much savings as you can while you're pregnant, before any unexpected costs start piling up, is just plain smart.

Find Out How Much Leave You're Allowed to Take

If you're planning to return to work after your baby is born, find out how much leave you're allowed to take by checking with your HR department or company ahead of time. Some states stipulate how much time you are allowed, and companies have their own policies on when you're eligible for leave, how much they offer, and whether that time off is paid. Determining how much pay you'll receive is pretty crucial, as losing income, even for a little bit, can have a major effect on some households—especially with those hospital expenses and new costs coming in. If you know how much leave you get and how much of that is paid, you can factor it in to your overall plan.

Add Baby to Your Health Plan ASAP

First and foremost, once that bundle of joy is born, make sure you add them to your health insurance plan. You usually have thirty to sixty days to do this, depending on your provider. No matter what, don't miss the window. A baby's medical appointments will start during week one, and you want your insurance to be on the hook for those pricey visits—not you.

Don't forget the health savings accounts we discussed in chapter 1. These can count toward your kids' health needs in addition to your own—think about how many copays you can cover with all those pretax dollars!

Make Sure You're All Set with Life Insurance

It's not just about you anymore! Bringing a baby into the world means you have to think about taking care of that kid, no matter what happens. This is a good time to make sure you have adequate life insurance so if something happens to you, your husband, or even both of you, your child's needs will be met.

And if you're going to be staying home while your husband serves as the primary breadwinner—or vice versa—you want to make sure that both parent and child will be covered financially if your family's sole income disappears. How much should you purchase? It's a good idea to have six to eight times your household's gross income in life insurance.

If you already have life insurance set up (excellent work, by the way!), make sure to adjust your beneficiaries. Your spouse can of course remain your primary beneficiary, but now you can add your child as a contingent, making them next in line.

Think about the Cost of Childcare

Childcare can be extremely expensive, so factor it into your budget, and see what you need to do to make it work. You may find that the cost of a nanny or day-care center will take a huge chunk out of your take-home pay, making staying home to provide care yourself worthwhile.

Outside of major metropolitan areas, you could end up spending $4,000–$9,000 per year on care. If you're in a major city, expect childcare to cost anywhere from $12,000 to $15,000 per year. If you know you're not going to stop working, keep these cost averages in mind, and try to pad your savings accordingly.

Retirement Savings

If you're going to be leaving the workforce, let's not forget about retirement savings. Yes, your husband will be working and probably contributing to his 401(k), but what about you?

As we discussed in the previous chapter, nowadays, it's a lot harder to support a family in retirement when just one person has been contributing to their fund. If you're married and staying home to take care of the household, you can still make *spousal IRA contributions*. While IRA contributions usually need to be made with earned income and in your own name, with a spousal IRA, you can contribute up to $5,500 a year. Think about the impact of this savings over time; it can make a huge difference in your quality of life postretirement.

Saving for College

It may be hard to imagine now, but someday that tiny bun in your oven may go off to college—a huge expense. You may even want to send them to an expensive private college prep school beforehand to ensure the best start. Either way, it's never too early to prepare, and the good news is there are many options available to help you do just that. Here are three great account types that can help you save for education-related costs.

529 plans, or "qualified tuition plans," were first developed to help families save for college. They're tax-advantaged plans, allowing you to invest money toward your child's education and earn interest on those investments tax free. You can even start before your baby arrives, putting the account in your name and transferring it to your child once they are born and assigned a Social Security number.

With the recent tax reform, these funds can be used for more than just college: starting in 2018, you can use up to $10,000 of 529 savings per year for K–12 tuition as well.

529 plans are a great choice for families who don't necessarily have a lot of investment experience, as the options are very simplistic. Rather than worrying about all the considerations that come with managing investments, you just choose from a range of investment strategies: aggressive, moderately aggressive, moderate, moderately conservative, or conservative.

If you're still unsure of what to pick, it's good to think about how much time your money will have to grow before you have to pay tuition. For example, if you're planning to send your child to public school and use the account for college expenses, you have eighteen years to invest. You don't have to worry about being particularly conservative right away because if the market drops in value during year one, you still have seventeen more to go. Plus, chances are, the future market won't be lower than it is right now, so being aggressive is totally appropriate.

In fact, you can continue to be aggressive up until about five years before your child is due to start college. By then, you've done a lot of the work. You've invested for thirteen years, steadily making contributions, and likely built up a significant chunk of change. Now it's time to start protecting those assets. From this point on, every year, you can move 20 percent into a conservative or moderately conservative fund. By the time the child is one year away from starting college, 80 percent of your funds should be invested conservatively. That way, if the markets do hit a rocky patch, you're covered.

Each state has a 529 plan, but you don't have to choose your own state's fund. You can select any plan you want, comparing costs and investment choices to find the right one for you. You also don't have to send your child to school in the state from which you purchase your plan—they can attend any school in the US.

However, keep in mind that all the tax-deferred growth associated with these plans occurs at the federal level. State taxes still apply, so if you find a plan in another state that seems more appealing, make sure you're not hurting yourself on the tax side of things. Some states offer a tax benefit for choosing their plan, which may make it worthwhile to buy in the state where you reside. For example, if you live in California and purchase a California 529 plan, you can pull funds out tax free.

But what if your child doesn't want to go to college? What if they want to become an entrepreneur out of high school or tour the country with their wildly successful rap trio?

Again, you've got options. If you have another child, they can become the beneficiary on the account. If you only have one kid, don't worry. Only the earnings—not what you've invested in the account—will be taxed at a 10 percent penalty if you withdraw them. There are also exceptions. If your child gets a scholarship, or if something happens to them that makes college out of the question, you can request a penalty-free withdrawal.

As of 2019, the annual 529 plan contribution limit for an individual is $15,000. If you're married, you can double that, putting away $30,000 each year toward educational expenses. Anything you contribute over that amount will trigger a federal gift tax. However, there is a specific exception for 529 plans: you can contribute up to five times the contribution limit within a five-year period without triggering the gift tax—$75,000 if you're single and $150,000 if you're married. If grandma and grandpa want to help out, the same rules apply.

One important thing to note: 529 plans are very strict in terms of what the funds can cover; while tuition and fees are definitely allowed, when it comes to an expense such as room and board, it depends on what you choose to do. On-campus housing and a school-sanctioned meal plan are permissible, but if you decide on costlier off-campus housing, you may need to make up the difference with other funds. And while you can use 529 funds to purchase the books on your child's reading list, an extra study guide or anything deemed unnecessary is subject to a penalty. You also can't use 529 plan dollars for equipment if the school doesn't explicitly require it. Once you start spending, keep receipts, because you'll have to prove that they were used on eligible expenses.

Education savings accounts are another way to save for college expenses. The real benefit of an education savings account used to be that you could use it for primary and secondary school tuition, while 529 plans only allowed for college expenses. However, now that 529 plans can be used for both, there are fewer advantages here.

Education savings accounts come with a contribution limit of $2,000 per year until the child's eighteenth birthday—something to take into account if you want to invest more than that per year. Otherwise, many of the same rules that govern a 529 plan apply to education savings accounts: if the beneficiary doesn't use it, it can be transferred to another child; all earnings used for education expenses are tax free; and if you end up withdrawing for a reason unrelated to education, those earnings are taxed at a 10 percent penalty.

With lower contribution limits and similar stipulations, it may seem like this type of account isn't worthwhile, but if you're someone who understands the markets and wants to actively manage the way your money is invested, this might be the route for you. Education savings accounts are entirely self-directed. You can buy Apple stock, Facebook stock—whatever you want. The choice is yours, making it more appealing for some.

The second benefit of education savings accounts is that they allow you to spend your earnings on a broader range of expenses, whereas 529 plans are far stricter.

Custodial accounts are worth considering if you think your kid may be the next Bill Gates and you don't want to pay the 10 percent penalty on earnings. This is just like a normal investment account. Rather than choosing from a set of general investment strategies, you invest in whatever you like, whether it's stocks, mutual funds, exchange-traded funds (ETFs)—it's all up to you.

With a custodial account, the assets are in the child's name, but as the custodian, you have full control of the funds. Once the child turns eighteen, you'll drop off, and the account is solely your off-spring's. The annual contribution limits are the same as those for a 529—$15,000 for a single person and $30,000 for a couple. Because it's not an education or college savings account, you can make withdrawals anytime for any purpose, as long as those withdrawals actually benefit the beneficiary (meaning you can't just use the funds to purchase a whole new wardrobe).

With this account, the first $1,050 of earnings are tax free, and any additional earnings are taxed at a reduced rate.

Bringing a baby into the world is one of the most life-changing things you can do, but paying for all the associated costs doesn't have to be stressful. When it comes to fitting a baby into your budget, just thinking about that extra step savings-wise can make everything less overwhelming. Every little bit helps, and using the tools we discussed here—and in previous chapters—can make a big difference.

Consider the financial impact of your choices, whether you're thinking about paying for childcare or providing it yourself. Establishing a robust emergency fund, utilizing health savings accounts, continuing to save for retirement, and evaluating all your options to plan for educational expenses can help set you up to comfortably manage the costs that inevitably come up and avoid some of the financial strain kids can bring on. With a strong plan in place, you'll be ready for anything family life throws at you—baby food, boogers, and anything else.

> Bringing a baby into the world is one of the most life-changing things you can do, but paying for all the associated costs doesn't have to be stressful.

Chapter 7

FINANCIAL DIY

W ant to explore the wild and wonderful world of capital markets? Whether you're interested in investments but don't know where to start or you've dabbled a little and want to go further, this chapter is for you. I'll give you the background—a quick Investments 101—and then show you what else is out there so when you're ready to take things up a notch, you have the information and tools you need. If you've got a strong understanding of the basics, feel free to skip to part II of this chapter!

Part I: The Basics

First, let's lay the groundwork and begin with the basics. Maybe you've heard about stocks, bonds, and the like, but you don't quite know what they actually are. No worries—you're not alone, and this is the perfect time to learn. We'll start with a handful of key concepts.

THE SKINNY ON STOCKS

When a business is looking to raise capital to fund activities such as hiring more employees or upgrading equipment, it may issue stock to bring in the dollars it needs. When you buy a company's stock— also referred to as an *equity security*—you become a part owner of that business, meaning it's possible to own a small part of some of the brands you love.

Besides owning a piece of the pie, what's so great about stocks?

Well, the stock market tends to trend upward, meaning that the money you invest is likely to grow over time. In addition, some companies also issue dividends, essentially giving a share of their profits directly to shareholders. Dividends are either declared monthly or quarterly and are usually paid out a month after they're announced, so if you play your cards right, you'll have more money in your pocket—or account—to play with or put toward a particular goal.

WHEN TO BUY

You probably already know that when it comes to the stock market, timing matters. So when's the best time to buy? A number of factors typically give investors the green light to purchase stocks. Low unemployment, an increase in the gross domestic product (GDP), low interest rates, and lower taxes all create an environment in which businesses are likely to thrive, and that means their stocks will grow as well. The inverse is also true: if these factors are heading downhill and unemployment, interest rates, and taxes are all high, buying stocks may not be a good idea.

This is pretty intuitive, too, if you think about it. If the unemployment rate is high, there are fewer people out there spending—they're probably saving the cash they have and looking for jobs instead. If taxes are higher, discretionary income is lower, so people have less money to work with, and many businesses are likely to fare worse. If the GDP is down, then we're not producing as much as a country, so stocks may not be growing. Keep in mind that these are just rules of thumb. Sometimes, the opposite of what you might expect happens—more on that in a minute.

THE UNDENIABLE VALUE OF DIVERSITY

We know that variety—or diversity—is the spice of life, and investing in stocks is no different. You may have heard stories from older generations—grandparents or great-grandparents—about how the company they worked for crashed and they lost their entire 401(k). That didn't happen because the account itself suddenly went bust when the company did; it happened because they invested all their funds in just one stock, their employer's, essentially putting all their eggs in one basket.

> We know that variety—or diversity—is the spice of life, and investing in stocks is no different.

Many people don't know any better. They think that because they work for a particular company, it's a good idea to invest everything in that organization. But if you do that for thirty years and the business goes belly up one day, it means all your savings are gone too. Diversifying your stock portfolio will keep your hard-earned savings safe and working for you. Here are five different options.

Blue-chip stocks. Blue-chip stocks are generally household names—companies such as Disney and Coca-Cola. They're large companies that have been around for decades, and they usually have a good reputation.

Blue chips are pretty steady. For instance, Disney usually hovers around $100 a share. If it does climb, Disney will usually do a stock split, dividing the shares to bring the price back to around $100 a pop.

Growth stocks. These companies are expected to grow more aggressively than blue chips, particularly because growth is the primary focus—think Amazon or Google. Rather than paying you in the form of dividends, companies focused on growth will take their profits and reinvest them in the business so they can grow even faster. Instead of taking the form of a monthly or quarterly payment, all your appreciation is going to show up in the share price.

Growth stocks are generally very volatile—you'll see lots of ups and downs. A particular share price may jump 7 percent one day and drop 3 percent the next. As such, there's a strong probability that you'll get a high return, but the chance for losses is significant too.

Cyclical stocks. Cyclical stocks are closely correlated to normal business and economic cycles. These are businesses offering a product or service that people buy when the economy is doing well and skip when things get tricky. Housing companies, auto manufacturers, and appliance manufacturers are all examples. As such, these are good bets when things are trending up economically.

Countercyclical stocks. Countercyclical stocks function in exactly the opposite way that cyclical stocks do (as you may have guessed). Gold is a perfect example. When the economy isn't doing very well, the price of gold shoots up, and as soon as things start to turn around, it drops. Budget retailers such as Walmart are also part of this group.

Defensive stocks. Food, pharmaceuticals, tobacco, these are items people buy no matter what the economy's doing. You still have to eat and take your prescription medication whether or not society is on stable ground financially. As such, you usually won't see any large swings here, making defensive stocks a pretty stable holding most of the time.

THE BRIEFING ON BONDS

Bonds are loans. When you buy a bond, you're lending a business your money for a set period. In return, the company agrees to pay you a certain amount of money per month—called a coupon—and at the end of that set period, they'll pay you the original purchase price. At the outset, or initial offering, you'll receive a list of the bond terms, the percentage coupon, and the length of the agreement. For instance, you might purchase a bond for $10,000, with the stipulation that the company will pay you back your $10,000 in five years and that you'll receive a monthly coupon of three percent—netting you some extra cash along the way. So every month that you hold the bond, you will get the 3 percent in the form of a $25 coupon payment. After three years, you would not only get your $10,000 investment back but also an additional $900 in coupon payments.

You also have the option to buy bonds in the secondary market, and when you do, you have the opportunity to purchase at a discount or a premium, which is directly correlated with current interest rates. So if the original bond offered by the company is being sold by someone else at a discount, that probably means that you could get a higher coupon if you went directly to the business and bought a new bond.

If the coupon is not as high as what you could get in the market right now, to compensate that secondary market seller might offer the bond at a cheaper price—say $900 instead of the company's initial offering of $1,000—making up for the loss in the coupon. Similarly, if a bond was originally sold with a 4 percent coupon, but the new rate is 2 percent, the secondary market will reflect that premium. Rather than selling at $1,000, the bond may cost you $1,300 to account for the higher monthly coupon you'll get.

Companies issuing bonds are rated by credit agencies such as Standard & Poor's or Moody's, and their ratings indicate whether they are likely to default based on their history. Bonds are rated from

AAA all the way down to DD. Think of the rating as equivalent to a grade on a paper. If a particular company has a DD rating, they haven't paid back some of their bonds in the past. If you notice that a bond you're interested in is paying a very high coupon—so high that it seems too good to be true—check out their rating. You may find the reason is a less-than-ideal history. With that high coupon, they may be acknowledging that they messed up in the past, and thus recognizing the risk inherent in purchasing from them. You have to decide if you're willing to take on that risk or whether you'd rather go with an AAA bond that's offering a smaller coupon but has never missed a payment.

Bonds are issued by governments, municipalities, and businesses. When thinking about whom to purchase from, there are a few things to consider.

Government bonds

Government bonds are by far the safest bonds you can get—because the government guarantees them and you don't have to worry that the government is going to go out of business. You can bet that if you lend the government $10,000 for five years, they're going to pay you back. Since they know that they're good for their money and that they're well trusted, their coupon is not going to be as high as the ones you'll get from riskier bonds. These bonds are also taxed at a federal level but not at the state level.

Municipal bonds

States, counties, and cities issue municipal bonds to cover everyday costs and capital projects. Maybe your city wants to put up a toll road, but they don't have the money to finance it. The government will issue bonds to complete the road and pay you back with a coupon generated from the road's toll income. Your coupon will usually be higher than the one you'd get from a government bond and it's also tax free—all that income is yours to keep. Because municipalities don't have quite the same guaranteeing power as the federal government, these bonds are considered moderately risky.

Corporate bonds

Corporate bonds are the riskiest options—since they're businesses, it's quite possible that they could fail. To compensate for this fact, they also offer the highest coupons, playing on the concept of risk and reward. What happens if the business fails?

Let's go back to our Disney example. Say that in addition to your Disney stock, you also buy some Disney bonds, but then Disney goes out of business. What then?

Well, there's an order of asset distribution. If a company goes under, the first thing it has to do is pay taxes; Uncle Sam always comes first. Then it's bondholders. Next, the shareholders—those who have stock in the company—will be paid. But neither stocks nor bonds are guaranteed; they're only paid out if there's enough money to cover them after the government gets its share. So if the company only has enough money to pay its taxes, everyone else is out of luck. If there is enough to pay taxes and bondholders, shareholders lose. This is definitely worth keeping in mind as you consider what to purchase.

MUTUAL FUNDS

Mutual funds remove all the work of diversification. Instead of doing it yourself, you're trusting a manager to do it for you. For instance, if you're interested in technology, but you don't know which technology stocks to buy, you can buy a technology mutual fund, and once you do, you'll be holding hundreds of technology stocks in your hot little hands—and be totally diversified.

Sound perfect? There are a few downsides. For one, because you're technically paying someone to choose for you, mutual funds can have high fees. In addition, mutual funds price after close of business, which is 1:00 p.m. Pacific time, so you are not able to trade in and out during stock market hours.

EXCHANGE-TRADED FUNDS

ETFs are very similar to mutual funds, but ETFs tend to have lower fees. Why? Rather than paying a manager to do the research and determine the best investments, companies offering ETFs track various indexes and select stocks based on that alone. For instance, a tech ETF may be buying the top 150 tech companies—and that's it. ETFs also trade like stocks, meaning if you want to trade during market hours, from 6:30 a.m. to 1:00 p.m. Pacific time, you can do so instantly and see the fund's price in real time. With these two factors in mind, if you're trying to choose between mutual funds and ETFs, I'd go with the latter.

GETTING STARTED

With the basics down pat, it's time to put your money where your mouth is! First you'll need a brokerage account. While your bank may have an investment option available, you may have to go through an advisor—making fees higher. Look for a self-trading investment platform instead. You can open one of these with companies such as

Charles Schwab, Fidelity, or E-Trade. Accounts can be opened and completely funded online, making it super easy to get started.

All set? Let's go over some crucial tips to keep you in the know as you begin investing.

SATISFY YOUR ORDER

When it comes to your brokerage account, you also want to think about how you'll pay for the stock you purchase. Say you open your account and you want to purchase ten shares of a particular stock but you only have enough money in the account to cover five. With stocks, you have five days to get the cash. You can pop a check in the mail with the knowledge that it will get to Schwab or other trading platform in two days and be in your account in three and breathe easy.

This little tip helped me out in a big way once. It was late—after hours—and I was trading in a rush. I placed the order, entering the number of shares based on the cash available in my account. But by the end of the day the stock price had risen, and I didn't have enough to cover the shares.

When I saw my account balance drop into the negative range, I totally freaked out. But then it clicked. I had five days to cover it. I wrote a check and sent it in without having to worry that I'd lose out on the purchase or be penalized. As long as you can cover the cost of what you've purchased within the five-day window, you're good to go.

With mutual funds and ETFs, however, you only have a two-day window to pay for your purchases, so make sure you're not buying something you can't cover ASAP!

THINK ABOUT TAXES

If you've saved some money on the side and you're interested in investing, you need to think about taxes. Every time you buy and sell securities, it's a taxable event. If you've made $5,000 on a particular holding, you may want to cash in, but you need to recognize that you'll need to pay taxes on your gains. Now keep in mind, this is only for nonretirement funds. If you are using retirement funds in an IRA, Roth, or other retirement account, you don't pay tax on earnings.

Securities are subject to two types of tax, and the rate you pay depends on how long you've held a particular stock and how much you make. If you've held the position for longer than twelve months, then you get to pay long-term capital gains—0, 15, or 20 percent depending on your income. If you make less than $38,600, your tax is 0. If you earn more than that, you'll pay either 15 or 20 percent, depending on your income and whether you're married. Just do a quick internet search for "long-term capital gains tax rate" along with the current year to determine how much you owe.

If you have held shares for less than a year, you'll be paying short-term capital gains—ordinary income tax. Those earnings will be taxed at the same rate as your income. Those can really sneak up on you if you're not mindful because you're paying it all out at the end of the year, so make sure you're tracking how much you earn—and accordingly, how much you'll owe—when you trade.

DON'T WANT TO DIY? NO WORRIES

Does do-it-yourself investing seem more like a stressful dream than something fun? No worries! If you've got extra cash and you want to invest, but you don't want to deal with the details, you have a couple of options.

First, you can get a financial advisor. They can talk you through your goals and help you handle every aspect of your financial life. Sounds great, right?

But what about the cost for full-service support like that? You're usually looking at about 1 to 2 percent of your portfolio value. That's quite a bit of money to pay. If you have half a million dollars, own a few properties, and own a couple of different types of accounts, it might be worth the expense. But if you don't have any significant financial planning needs, with anywhere from $10,000 all the way up to $300,000 or $400,000 in the bank, you don't necessarily need to pay the price for an advisor. A lower-cost option is using an automated investing platform.

These can be great, and that's why I've started my own with the help of Charles Schwab: Nummata.com. Getting started is super simple. You head to the website and take a risk tolerance test. With a few quick questions, the platform determines what kind of risk you're willing to take on and presents you with three different portfolios to choose from based on your results. You can then open your account and fund it right there on the spot.

At that point, the algorithms behind the scenes take over, investing your cash and rebalancing your portfolio on the regular. That means if you have five different investments and three of them have grown by 50 percent, the algorithm will make sure to capture that profit and redistribute it so that your whole portfolio is growing. And if you've got a taxable account, it will make sure your tax benefit is maximized, too, ensuring that any gains are offset by losses. Once it's all in the works, you don't even have to click a button—everything's done for you.

You get all the benefits of having an advisor at a fraction of the cost—just 0.35 percent, yes, less than half a percent! If you invest $100,000, your fee is just $350 per year, versus the $1,000 or $2,000 an advisor would charge. That means you're retaining more of your returns.

Part II: Go Further

If you're well aware of stocks, bonds, mutual funds, and more, and you're ready to try something new, there are plenty of other options.

REAL ESTATE INVESTMENT TRUSTS

A REIT is a portfolio of real estate. The people running the funds are actually buying hard assets such as strip malls or hospitals, locations that will incur rent or can be flipped for a profit, which is then paid out to investors. And just like with stocks, as a shareholder, you own a real piece of the pie—in this case, property—further diversifying your portfolio.

Also, REITs customarily pay high dividends; the IRS requires that all REITs pay out at least 90 percent of their income to shareholders. So while you might get a 1.5 percent dividend from a Disney stock, you can get something like 10 percent from a REIT.

But REITs also have a potential downside. Risk is part of the game, and I can give you a real-life example. I invested in a REIT that was purchasing healthcare buildings—assisted-living centers, hospice facilities, and hospitals. A portion of these assets came from a government assisted-living facility, and right after the REIT bought the building and added it to the portfolio, that government budget got cut. The projected 10 percent dividend was slashed to reflect the fact that the new building wouldn't produce the expected income.

If you're investing in a REIT that is purchasing shopping centers and a few of the tenants go out of business, you may find yourself in a similar position. If that rental income isn't coming in, your dividend won't be as high—yet another reason to protect yourself via diversity!

STOCK OPTIONS

With stock options, you're buying or selling *the option* to buy or sell a stock. For example, if you want to buy one hundred shares of a particular stock, you can set your price by saying that you don't want to buy it right now, but you want the option to purchase it later if it hits a particular price. You enter into an agreement with someone who has the stocks and is willing to sell them if they hit your desired rate. But you also pay a price just for the option to make the purchase—maybe it's $1.25 per share just for the option to buy. This is called a call option.

The same goes for selling. Maybe you have Bank of America stock valued at $99, and you don't want to sell it now, but if it goes up just a bit—to $103—you'd be willing to sell it. This is called a put option.

If you buy a call, you're buying the option to buy a stock. If you sell a call, you are selling the option to buy a stock. If you buy a put, you're buying the option to sell a stock, and if you sell it, you're selling the option to sell a stock.

If you sell, you're getting paid—someone will pay you that premium for the option to buy or sell—and vice versa; if you're buying the option, you're paying it out.

FUTURES

Futures are just like options, except with these, you're not buying the option, you're committing. You're saying, "I'm going to buy this stock six weeks from now at this price."

STRATEGIES TO EMPLOY

Now let's cover some concepts and strategies to employ. Combined with the information you have on types of investments, these methods can make you feel like a pro.

Shorting Stocks

Shorting stocks is an alternative method if you want to get in on the stock game. This is where you have a bear mindset: you believe that the stock market is going to go down (as opposed to a bull mindset, where you believe the stock market is going to go up). Here, you're not actually buying; you're borrowing. In doing so, you're taking on debt (also known as a short position) with the hope that the stock price will drop—at which point, you'll buy the shares and keep the difference.

So if a stock is trading at $50 per share and you short one hundred shares, then if the price drops to $40 per share, you'll buy them and pay $40 per share for a total of $4,000. You've just made $1,000 because you borrowed shares at $50 per share, and you get to keep the proceeds.

There are downsides here. If you borrow the stock and the price keeps going up, eventually you have to close the position, meaning if the price per share goes up to $60 and doesn't drop, you'll have to pay the share price. A great example of this can be seen in the 2015 movie *The Big Short*, where the protagonist recognized that banks were lying and creating a housing bubble that would eventually burst. He began shorting stocks, eventually making his investors millions when it did.

Using Orders

Typical stock purchasing is called a market order—you decide you want to buy a stock and you do it. But other types of orders are available.

Limit order. A limit order allows you to buy or sell a security at a specific price or better. You enter the price, and that becomes the limit order. The stock will not be added to your account unless it can be purchased at the price you specify.

Stop order. Stop orders are another option. By using one, you're trying to protect yourself from significant losses by triggering a sale the moment it hits a particular low. If the price of a position drops by a set amount or more, the stop order will trigger it to be sold automatically.

There is a key difference between limit orders and stop orders. While with a limit order, you get the price you set, with a stop order, the sale of your stock is triggered when the stock hits a certain price, and then you get the next available price. For instance, though a stop order may be triggered at $97.00, you may get $96.98 if that's the next price the stock hits.

So why are there two different kinds? Wouldn't a limit order always be the best option? Since limit orders require a set price, it's possible that the purchase or sale will never execute. If the price dips below your set amount without hitting it, you then miss out on the opportunity to make the deal, even if you could have gotten it for a cent more or less. You're essentially saying, "I want this exact price, or I don't want it at all."

Meanwhile, with a stop order, you're saying that you'll accept the variability and accordingly, the risk. In a large market downturn, the stop order could be placed at $97, but if the market's tumbling fairly quickly, it may not execute until shares are at $87. The potential for variation is much higher.

Both of these order types can either be good for the day or good until canceled—meaning that your order remains in existence until you cancel it. Sometimes, depending on the platform you use, a limit of sixty to ninety days may be used.

Margin

Margin allows you to buy stocks with up to double the amount of cash you have in your account—kind of like buying stocks on credit. If you open an account with $100,000 and use margin, you'll have $200,000 to play with. These accounts can also be used for short sales, and they track exactly what you've borrowed, limiting the amount available to you.

Margin is good for when you want to try to fast-forward your return; you can do a lot more with $200,000 than you can with $100,000. But there is no real purpose—it's just a feature that allows you to take on extra credit to go out there and make investments.

You also want to be careful because if you're leveraging half your account, you can wipe yourself out if you don't play your cards right. If you're just getting into stocks and bonds, margin is probably not for you. But if you have experience trading stocks, bonds, mutual funds, and ETFs, and have dabbled in options, margin could be step three.

Efficient Market Hypothesis

There are a number of different schools of thought out there on how to invest. Picture the process of picking stocks as throwing darts at a target. Some of them will hit the bull's eye; some of them won't. You don't really know which ones are going to be spot on—the efficient market hypothesis says that the same is true of the stock market.

This theory holds that it's impossible to beat the market because it is efficient: the share price that is established or released already has the latest news factored into it. By the time you find out that

Amazon killed its earnings, the company's share price is already going to reflect that insight. Thus, according to this theory, shares always trade at their fair market value. It's impossible to purchase undervalued stocks or sell stocks at inflated prices.

This is a great theory for someone who is a passive investor. If you believe you can't predict the markets and you don't want to try, that's okay. You know that overall, the market trends upward. With that knowledge, by the same token, your investment will increase in value over time. If the efficient market hypothesis resonates with you, Vanguard is a great investment choice. The firm is very passive, with a huge suite of funds that just track indexes.

Dollar-Cost Averaging

If you want to pick stocks based on your favorite companies—maybe you drink Starbucks so you want to invest there or you wear Lululemon so you think the brand might be a good choice—dollar-cost averaging your account is a good way to go. With this method, you don't put all your money in the market at the same time. Why?

If you put all your money in the market on Monday and it drops on Tuesday, the value of your investments declines all at once. Especially in times of volatility, when the market is all over the place, the last thing you want to do is invest everything you have at once.

With dollar-cost averaging, you space out your purchases. You decide that you'll invest on, say, the first of every month for a year, no matter what. That way, if there is any variation in price, you're going to be able to capture it over the period you selected. In theory, over time, you usually see that the share price you paid is lower than the market average.

No matter what method you choose, you should be up on the market so you can employ your strategies accordingly. So what should you track to stay on top of your investments and make the most informed choices possible? The following indexes can provide the insights you need:

- The S&P 500. The S&P 500 is the index of the top five hundred companies in the US.

- The Dow Jones Industrial Average. Another index that people usually watch—because it's indicative of how the overall market is doing—is the Dow Jones Industrial Average. This, however, is only made up of thirty stocks.

- The Russell 2000. This index is composed of the top two thousand smaller-sized companies.

KEEP YOUR GOALS IN MIND

If you're saving for a goal—such as paying for a wedding, buying a house, or covering your retirement costs—and you're not sure how to invest, the time frame can help you determine how to proceed. If you're in your twenties and saving for retirement, for example, be as aggressive as possible. You can't touch this money until you're fifty-nine and a half, so why hold cash or bonds? You might as well have all your funds in stock because you have plenty of time.

The further you are from your goal, the more aggressive you want to be. But as you get closer, you want to start scaling back your risk because the last thing you want is to lose your investment in a market downturn.

If you're saving for a shorter-term goal, you can play with how your funds are allocated so that a single scenario such as a market crash won't wipe you out. Here are some time frames and asset break-downs that can help dictate your portfolio.

If you are two to four years out from your goal, consider putting

- 42 percent in sector-specific investments or a mixture of large, medium, and small capitalized companies;

- 35 percent in bonds;

- 15 percent in cash; and

- 8 percent in international holdings.

And if you have more than four years to go, put

- 72 percent in sector-specific investments or a mixture of large, medium, and small capitalized companies;

- up to 15 percent in bonds;

- 13 percent in international stocks; and

- 0 percent in cash.

EXTRA CREDIT

Reading a Stock Chart

Ready for some extra credit? Let's talk about how to read those cool stock charts that show up in newspapers or when you're doing your investment research online. Some people believe that they can predict where their stocks will go based on the information these charts contain; however, this has not been proven. We'll take a look at each aspect of the chart, what it means, and how it can be helpful in determining your next move. Let's break things down using the following chart.[8]

---

8   "What's in a Stock Chart?," *Investors Business Daily*, accessed September 19, 2018, https://www.investors.com/ibd-university/chart-reading/chart-contents/.

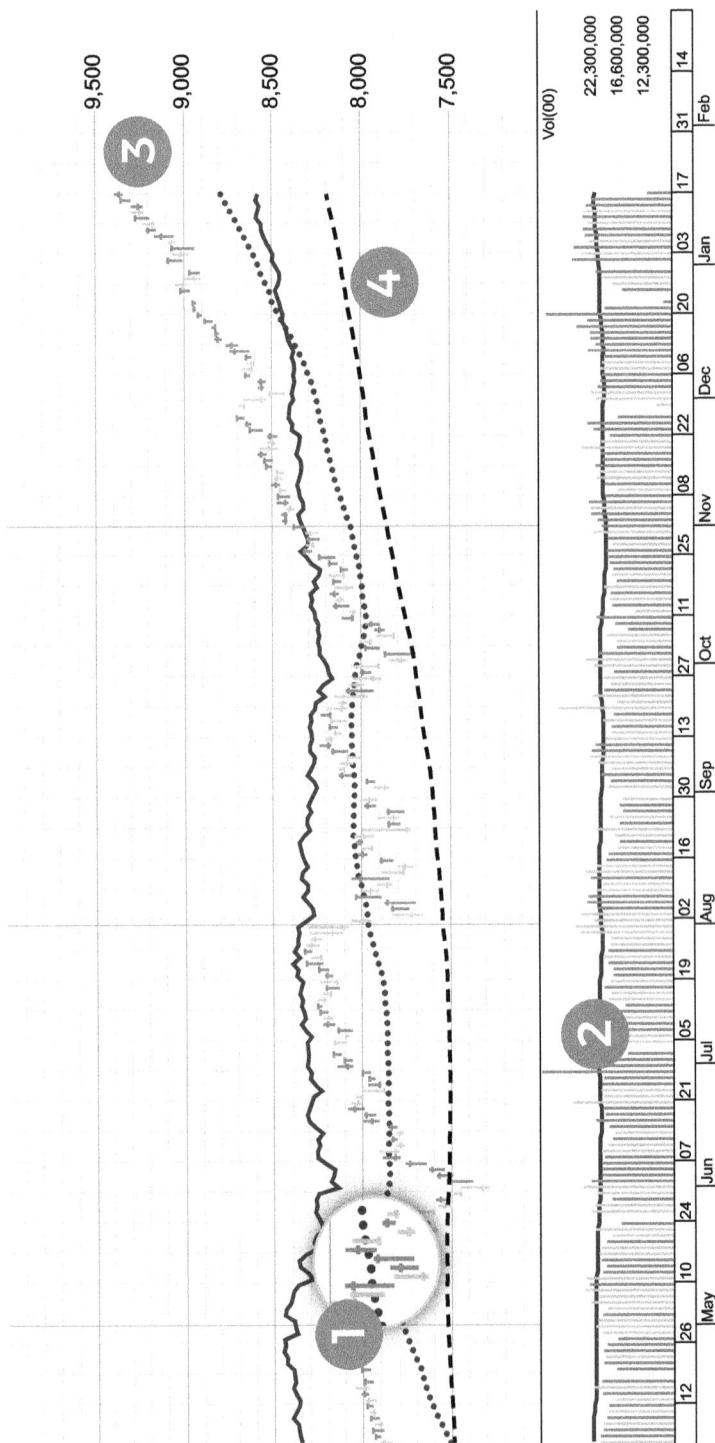

(It's important to note that stock charts document either daily or weekly movement. This one is highlighting the action that occurs over the course of a year.) Take a look at the little vertical lines in the magnified bubble labeled "1" in the image above. These show where the stocks were priced over the course of each month. The vertical line shows the high and low during the trading hours, and the horizontal slash indicates where they closed. The dotted lines indicate stocks that closed up, and the solid lines indicate stocks that closed down.

The lines running across the bottom of the chart, labeled "2," show volume—the number of shares traded over time—with dotted and solid indicating stocks that closed up or down, respectively. Why is volume important? It tells us which stocks are traded frequently and which don't see a lot of action. Stocks that aren't traded very often are referred to as "thinly traded," which indicates that there's not a huge market for them and that you might have trouble selling or buying. For novice investors, this isn't normally an issue because you're probably out there buying brand names—companies that are traded in the millions. It's only when you're purchasing relatively unknown or small companies that volume becomes a factor.

The solid and dashed lines running across the middle of the chart—that end at label "3"—track moving averages, or the share price over a set number of days. The solid line depicts the average share price over the past fifty days, while the dashed line depicts share price over the past two hundred days.

With these, we can get into a bit of chart theory. We can rationalize that based on these averages, a stock probably won't dip much below the lower of the two lines or soar much higher than the top line. As such, if your stock reaches the top of the range, it may be a good time to sell since it probably will not go much higher, whereas if it hits the bottom, it might be a good time to buy. However, this has not been proven to work every time (if it did, everyone would make millions in the market), but it's a good rule of thumb to keep in mind when exploring this trading methodology.

Now, check out "4": the dotted squiggly line. This shows you the S&P 500—the five hundred largest companies in the market—and how the stock is growing relative to it. If your entire portfolio is under this line, this means the holding is underperforming in comparison to the top five hundred companies in the market.

Bollinger Bands

Bollinger Bands are another popular strategy tied to moving averages, captured in the chart below. When you use Bollinger Bands, you'll only see one moving average line on the chart. (In the chart below, it's a twenty-one-day average, represented by the middle dashed line.) The upper and lower bands, or Bollinger Bands, are set two standard deviations higher and lower than the moving average, capturing volatility—and thus risk. According to the theory, the stock should stay within these bands. So if you want to try to time the market—just for fun—you might buy or sell based on whether the stock is nearing the upper or lower band.

Please keep in mind that this is just for your knowledge; I don't recommend that anyone who is just starting out try to use charts to trade because it doesn't always work. Touting your new insights over brunch, however, never fails to entertain.[9]

---

9   "Bollinger Band," Investopedia, accessed September 19, 2018, https://www.investopedia.com/terms/b/bollingerbands.asp.

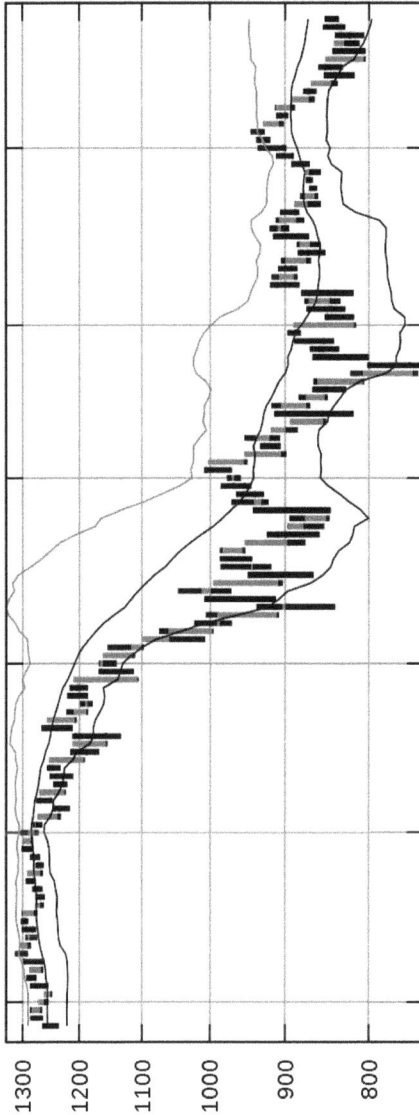

Source: Bollinger Capital.

Using the information in this chapter, you've created and/or diversified your portfolio and you're armed with the insights to make your investments work for you. Now it's time to put your knowledge to work and reap the benefits: successfully #adulting and achieving your savings goals one day at a time.

Chapter 8

BEYOND FINANCES: SELF-CARE STRATEGIES TO KEEP YOU SUCCESSFUL, HAPPY, AND SANE

If you've taken the time to read this book, you're probably interested in improving yourself, making sure you're on the right track, and being prepared. I can relate—self-improvement has been a huge passion of mine for as long as I can remember, and I'm always looking for ways to get better. I also like change; if something seems static in my life, you can bet I'll be working to create that transformation myself.

I've tried all kinds of techniques, from hydration to meditation, to try to get a better handle on my goals and dreams. In the process, I've uncovered ten go-to strategies that have helped me stay focused and driven. So let's finish off by taking a moment to look at the big picture: while your finances are important, you're so much more than your bank account. And while we've covered lots of strategies to get your money in order, it's crucial to make sure your mind and body are set up for success too. Life's not a sprint—it's a marathon. If you commit to working on and taking care of yourself, that finish line is yours for the taking. The following tactics have helped me stay on pace. I think they might just work for you too.

> While your finances are important, you're so much more than your bank account.

Five to Thrive

We all go through periods when we feel super stressed or where there's so much going on that we find ourselves wondering how we'll cope with it all. Maybe it's a series of tight deadlines you don't know how you'll make, a job switch that's throwing you for a loop, or a long-term relationship that's just not working the way it used to. When you feel like the pressure is on and you can't breathe—no matter the circumstances—"five to thrive" is here to help you out.

While there will always be a limited amount of room in our personal buckets, the reserves we draw on to get it all done, this is one way to counter the stress and make a bit more space for all you need to do. Here's how it works.

Choose five simple things that make you feel happy and whole and commit to doing them at least three times per week. Your five things shouldn't cost much, if anything at all, but they'll keep you stable and sane in rocky times when everything else seems out of whack. My five to thrive are below, in case you need some inspiration.

A daily Starbucks trip

I've mentioned this before, but the whole Starbucks experience is so calming for me. When life gets crazy, I make sure to include a Starbucks trip as part of my morning routine. Something about driving there, walking through the door, ordering that perfect cup of coffee, and slowly sipping it on my way to work makes it seem like all is right with the world, if even for just a few moments!

- I also mentally prepare for the day during this time or acknowledge my top priorities. Consider carving out a little "me time" in the form of a coffee run or some other break that you can count on for a few minutes of chill amid the chaos of life.

Planning out my weeks

As you may have guessed, I love to plan. I also like to do it on paper—writing everything out helps me visualize my schedule and prioritize properly so that I can tackle my tasks with confidence.

- Since putting pen to paper is such an important part of the process for me, there's nothing more motivating than a cute planner. Just cracking open the binding makes me happy. If you think a planner might improve your day-to-day experience, don't underestimate the power of decorating! I always take my planner personalization to the next level with stickers. This is not the place to worry about silliness—if it makes you feel good, do it!

Working out

The benefits of exercise are so much more than losing weight or toning up. Tons of studies have shown that exercise is one of the best ways to combat anxiety and let off steam—with the added effect of boosting your mood and energy levels. I can vouch for that: I always leave my workouts less stressed than when I started them. As such, hitting the gym at least three times per week is a crucial part of my five to thrive.

Meditation

Meditation is such a great way to stay focused and relaxed, and you don't need to devote a lot of time to it to feel the results. I use a really cool app called Headspace. Headspace offers meditations to address all kinds of issues and interests, whether I want to fall asleep faster or get motivated for a big meeting. And having a guide right there in my palm means I can take a second to tune in no matter where I am or what I'm doing.

- I simply pop in my headphones, pull up the meditation I want, and dedicate five or ten minutes to listening to myself and cutting out all that extra noise. After two months of consistent meditation—the app makes it easy to do this daily—I noticed extraordinary benefits, and it's become a staple of my routine.

Playing fetch with my dogs

Some quality time with my best furry buds never fails to lift my spirits—and I'm not alone. Studies show that people with pets usually have lower blood pressure, heart rates, and risk of heart disease than their petless peers. And recent research suggests that pets can be effective in relieving stress and anxiety.[10] Chasing your dog around your local park or cuddling up with your kitty and some Netflix can help combat any *scaries* you might be experiencing.

Don't Be Afraid to Seek Help

Life is hard, especially in your twenties and early thirties when you have so much going on. There's no reason to feel ashamed or embarrassed about needing some support. We all do. I've spent so much time replaying things over and over in my mind, wondering how I could have done something differently or better. Getting caught up in a downward spiral of self-deprecation is painful, and having someone to talk to can be a huge help.

> There's no reason to feel ashamed or embarrassed about needing some support.

---

10   Mandy Oaklander, "Science Says Your Pet Is Good for Your Mental Health," *Time*, April 6, 2017, http://time.com/4728315/science-says-pet-good-for-mental-health/.

A therapist can provide another perspective without being biased. Sometimes, saying it out loud to someone you trust—a person who has no skin in the game—is just what you need to manage stress and make it to the other side. And even when you're not in crisis mode, regular check-ins, where you have the chance to talk about anything that's on your mind, can do a world of good. You may even have an epiphany or two about what's next for you!

Try Toastmasters

Fear of public speaking—or glossophobia, if you want to get technical—is pretty common: about 25 percent of people report having it. And if you don't conquer this fear, it can definitely have an impact on your personal and professional success. It's so important to be able to share your awesome ideas with others. If you don't speak up, you could be missing out on exciting opportunities (and the rest of us will be denied your brilliance).

Toastmasters can help. An international organization with chapters all over the world, Toastmasters gives people the tools to improve their communication and leadership skills. With endless opportunities to practice giving speeches and learning skills to lead others, this awesome program is absolutely worth your time.

I've always been an introvert, and participating in Toastmasters took me out of my comfort zone in an important way. When I go to meetings consistently, I feel more confident overall. And every time I give a speech or lead a table topic, it feels like such a win.

Now, in addition to my newfound speech and leadership skills, I'm also better at speaking off the cuff, spontaneously at meetings and carrying on conversations. Toastmasters has refined the way I speak and the way I *feel* speaking in front of others—and that is priceless.

Give Back

Giving back isn't just about writing a check to a worthy organization. If you want to make a real difference, seek out nonprofits that align with your interests and areas of expertise. See if they have a board position available—where you can help direct the trajectory of the organization or determine how they fund their various projects—or just volunteer. In addition to the great work you'll be doing, you'll also benefit from the sense of giving and gratitude that comes with sharing your time and skills.

Often, you'll meet a great group of like-minded people in the process. Through my nonprofit work, I've been able to connect with some extraordinary women and have created a network with a slew of other perks. Through these connections, I've been able to get help and support with my own personal and professional projects and offer the same kind of support to others. I've gained at least as much, if not more, than I've given.

Read

It sounds simple enough, but reading regularly can make a big difference. First, absorbing the way someone else writes improves your vocabulary and helps you speak more eloquently. I always notice the difference between the words I use and the way I talk when I'm reading as opposed to when I'm not. If I get busy and can't pick up a book for a while, it's almost as if my facility with language gets worse.

What's another transformational opportunity when it comes to the written word? You'll expand your grasp of so many other fascinating topics and get a closer look at someone else's worldview to boot.

Take a Multivitamin

Popping a multivitamin may seem frivolous, but I assure you it's not. In addition to ensuring you get all kinds of must-have nutrients that your diet may lack, a multivitamin can have an impact on the way you feel.

I used to notice that in the afternoon—around 2:00 p.m.—I would start to get a bit sluggish. By then my morning cup of coffee would have worn off, and the hours would start to drag. I'd end up reaching for a second cup to make it through the rest of the day—even though, sometimes, it actually made me feel worse. But when I take a multivitamin, I see a real difference. My energy is sustained, and I don't need that extra afternoon jolt to stay engaged with tasks and projects. It's a little investment in your well-being that's totally worth it.

Create Rituals That Change with You

While the word *ritual* might seem a little *woo woo*, it's simply a set of behaviors performed regularly. Having rituals that are meant to maintain your health and happiness will help keep you strong, confident, and centered. Unlike five to thrive, these don't have to be nearly as frequent, as long as they're regular. For instance, I take a long soak in the tub and do a nice, thorough facial once a week. Every month, I set aside time to reflect on my goals and take the pulse of my personal progress. My rituals serve as a reminder that I'm worthy of my time and give me the extra *oomph* to get through any struggle I might be having.

Another important insight on rituals? Leave room to let them evolve as you change. You may find that you need to add something to your regimen that you hadn't thought of previously or that one of your rituals no longer serves you. You can—and should—give yourself room to adjust accordingly. The whole point is to do what works best for you, and that shifts throughout our lives.

Exercise!

This one may seem like a given (and is a key component of my five to thrive), but it can't be overstated: exercise is essential for your health, but it also just makes you feel good. It relieves stress, increases energy, and offers so many benefits that help you to be the best version of yourself.

If you haven't exercised in a while and you're getting back out there, you might feel tired at first—often more than before you started. But that's just your body adjusting. Give it some time, and that sleepy feeling will fade, along with tons of things that aren't serving you well.

Shoot for a Gallon of Water a Day

Many Americans are chronically dehydrated, and if you're one of them, chances are the lack of *agua* in your everyday life is also making you tired and irritable. You've probably heard that drinking eight glasses of water per day is the key to staying hydrated, but that's not really enough. In my experience, a gallon a day is really the perfect amount, keeping your cells quenched, flushing out toxins, and even raising your energy levels. (Now, bear in mind that I am five feet ten, so if you are significantly shorter, a gallon a day may be overkill.) It's also totally free if you treat yourself to a sweet reusable bottle to help track your intake and get drinking! Your mind, body, and perhaps even those who have been subject to your wrath will thank you.

Put Your Bare Feet on the Earth

This is not a metaphor, and I haven't lost my mind. I want you to actually walk outside without shoes or socks on and let those soles touch the ground. Maybe you were with me until this one, and now you're shaking your head, wondering what kind of Kool-Aid I've been drinking. But let me explain.

This process is called "earthing," and researchers have proven that it's no joke. When we're standing on a natural surface—soil, grass, or sand—our bodies have the opportunity to connect with the electrons in the earth.[11] Early studies have shown that making this connection can improve health in so many ways, from reducing pain to improving immunity and, of course, reducing stress.[12]

Our shoes and the sidewalk actually interrupt this process, so take the time to take a walk on the beach barefoot or step onto a grassy patch and feel the blades tickle your toes. This is just a small tip; it's not a magic bullet, and you won't necessarily feel a difference right away. But it's a little piece of self-care that just helps.

———

We work so hard in so many areas of our lives, giving our all to our jobs, our families, our friends—even our pets. Oftentimes, taking care of others comes so naturally, but we have to learn to take care of ourselves. I hope that at least a few of the strategies I've shared resonate and help you find a bit of serenity in the ups and downs that life can bring. Remember, the best investment

---

11   Isaac Eliaz, "The Surprising Health Benefits of Going Barefoot," MindBodyGreen, September 28, 2018, https://www.mindbodygreen.com/0-9099/the-surprising-health-benefits-of-going-barefoot.html.

12   Eliaz, "Surprising Health Benefits."

you can make is in yourself! If you're feeling cool and capable, you're going to slay the day, month, year, and everything else that comes your way.

And just like that, we're at the end of our time together. We've tackled so much, including the many personal and financial topics that tend to pop up in your twenties and beyond. I hope you'll find yourself coming back to these chapters as you need them—using these pages as a sort of choose-your-own-adventure guide to #adulting.

I know that finances can be scary, especially if this is your first rodeo. But by just showing up—and reading this book—you've already conquered the most important step to take control of your financial future and everything that comes with it. Now you have all the tools you need to make it happen. No matter what phase or stage you're in, I know you'll nail it! You've got this, and there are so many of us out there—me included—who have your back.

ABOUT THE AUTHOR

Ariana Mangum's love of finance began in college, when she joined a stock-trading challenge just for fun. While she didn't have much cash to play with back then, she was totally game to manage the fictional million-dollar portfolio her professor assigned. She was immediately enthralled by the ins and outs of capital markets and the rush of watching her stocks rise and fall. But what she found was more than a budding interest; it was a calling. Learning and helping others learn about investing and wealth management became her passion and her path.

Today, she is the cofounder and wealth planning manager of Miramontes Capital, a financial planning firm, and is the founder of Nummata.com, an online retirement investment platform. Along with the expert support and advice she provides to assist her clients in reaching their retirement goals, she is dedicated to helping young women successfully prepare for their financial futures—and everything else that lies ahead. A big believer in living life to its fullest and giving her all to everything she does, she's also an avid Spartan Racer and a loving dog mom.

ACKNOWLEDGMENTS

I would like to thank my dad, Don, for showing me what a strong work ethic is and for giving me an example to pursue my dreams. I'd also like to thank my mother, Wendy, for instilling an entrepreneurial mindset in me, teaching me how to build my own future and how to self-start. Thank you to my husband, Sid, for always pushing me to be the best version of myself, for being a mentor, and for always giving me unconditional love. To my sister, Angelena, thank you for showing me how to look at things from a positive perspective, and to my brother, Peter, for always inspiring me.

WORK WITH ARIANA

For financial planning and investment management, contact Miramontes Capital at (800) 460-1595.

For automated, do-it-yourself investing with professionally crafted portfolios, visit nummata.com.